WHEN THE GLASS SLIPPER DOESN'T FIT

CLAIRE CLONINGER
KARLA WORLEY

D0067229

New Hope® Publishers

Birmingham, Alabama

New Hope Publishers
P.O. Box 12065
Birmingham, AL 35202-2065
www.newhopepubl.com

Library of Congress Cataloging-in-Publication Data

Cloninger, Claire.
When the glass slipper doesn t fit / Claire Cloninger and Karla Worley.-- [Rev. ed.].
    p. cm.
ISBN 1-56309-437-1
1. Christian women--Religious life. I. Worley, Karla. II. Title.
BV4527 .C58 2000
248.8 43--dc21
    00-010104

Cover design by Rachael Crutchfield
Cover photo from VCG/FPG.

ISBN: 1-56309-437-1
N004129·0800·7.5M1

To Virginia and Charlie, my Mom and Dad,
who always found a way
to make expectations seem possible
and reality seem bearable.

Claire

To Dennis, Seth, Matt, and Ben,
whose presence in my life
is a constant reminder that reality
is the best fantasy of all.

Karla

CONTENTS

When I was a child,

I talked like a child,

I thought like a child,

I reasoned like a child.

When I grew up,

I put childish ways

behind me.

FIRST CORINTHIANS 13:11

1

UP TO MY ELBOWS—AND NO SIGN OF A PRINCE

Karla's chapter about things that just haven't turned
out the way they were supposed to

> *Living happily
> ever after wasn't
> original with
> Cinderella.
> It began
> with God.*
>
> —Beth Moore,
> *Breaking Free:
> Making Liberty
> in Christ
> a Reality in Life*

I spent most of 1989 throwing up. I don't mean to be offensive, but the second of my three children was born in November. That year, as my boys put it, I "hurled."

I was really looking forward to 1990. It was going to be the year I "got my act together" again. But I had forgotten what it is like to have a new baby. (God lets us forget—or else we might never have another one!) It turned out to be a long winter of long, cold nights with very little sleep. By the time spring came, I had put on twenty-five pounds of postpartum depression. I was fat, tired, and generally miserable. At a really low point, I wrote to my friend Claire:

I am not Karla. I am drill sergeant. I am backyard referee. I am chauffeur, cook, bottle-washer, nursemaid, bathroom monitor, accountant, and plumber. Not to mention that I am supposed to have enough of me left over to be friend, confidante, and colleague to my husband. And, oh, did I mention sexy?

I want to paint my nails. I want to go shopping. I want to curl up by the fire and read books. I want to sleep late. I want to have the energy to stay up late enough to see David Letterman. I don't want to have to buy industrial-strength concealer to hide the bags under my eyes. I don't want to shop in the Womans' World department . . . I want to shop in Juniors.

I'd like to be the witty, sparkling conversationalist I once was. I want to be spontaneous, attractive, and well dressed. I don't even recognize this dumpy, grumpy person I see in the mirror!

I feel like Cinderella must have felt, scrubbing baseboards and wood, knowing in her heart that she could be a princess, if only she had the dress, the shoes, and the time to do her hair.

Where is my fairy godmother? I could sure use that wand right now. I'd bop myself, my house, and my family,... and poof! My life would finally fall into place.

Claire's boys were both grown and had graduated. How I envied her long nights of uninterrupted sleep and her days full of freedom! Claire, ever a wise friend, didn't rub it in.

She wrote back with graciousness, sharing some of her own struggles with her writing career, with growing older, and with readjusting to downsizing her life and a suddenly empty nest.

Although Claire was at a different stage in her life, she, too, was having trouble coming to grips with who she was. She wrote, "I think the word I'm looking for is *surrender*—as in "giving up." Not giving up our dreams of finally being allowed to be "Claire" and "Karla." More like being willing to give up our ideas of who "Claire" and "Karla" really are.

Ten years later, Claire and I are at new places. My children are now in school, and I have gone back to work. Claire is a grandmother! But we still contend with these feelings of longing and frustration. All of us, at whatever stage in life we find ourselves, have discovered that reality doesn't always measure up to our expectations. ("If I could take off that last ten pounds... " "If I just made more money..." "If I only had more time..." "If I had a husband who would take out the trash...!") We wish for something more.

Let's face it, most of us grew up expecting to be Cinderella. We wanted the handsome prince, the fairy godmother, the horse-drawn carriage. When Lady Diana Spencer married Britain's Prince Charles, we were glued to the TV, fascinated with her because she had actually achieved our dream. (See, we knew all along it was possible!) Years later, after Diana's painful divorce and tragic death, we realize that even the life of a princess is not all it's cracked up to be. Still, we dream. In our hearts, we are the princess; it's just that these ungrateful pumpkins and mice we live and work with don't realize it.

Recently, my girlfriends and I spent a Saturday afternoon watching the Disney classic version of *Cinderella.* Talk about stages of life —we cover the gamut: a forty-four-year-old single executive; a forty-four-year-old wife/mother/writer; a thirty-five-year-old college advisor, married, with no children; a twenty-eight-year-old single health professional; a thirty-year-old single minister. But all of us were little girls again that afternoon. And I had a revelation.

Cinderella was content. And not just at the end of the story, when she had the glass slipper on her foot and the handsome prince by her side. Cinderella was content at the beginning, when she was up to her elbows in work, with no prince in sight! Sure she dreamed of going to the ball, but there she was scrubbing floors, *and she was singing!* Birds were twittering around her, the sun was shining brightly on the sill, and Cinderella beamed. Cinderella was as joyful and lovely scrubbing floors as she was with a crown on her head. Forget about the glass slipper; I want to know how she did that!

Although a fairy-tale princess and a New Testament preacher might not seem to have much in common, the apostle Paul had something of the same outlook as Cinderella. He put it this way: "I've learned by now to be quite content whatever my circumstances" (Phil. 4:12, *The Message*). Paul wrote these words from a prison cell. In that unlikely place he, like Cinderella, had found a reason to sing.

Suppose—just suppose—that you and I could learn to do this: to be content in whatever state we find ourselves. To sing while we scrub floors. To ignore the wallpaper we can't afford to change, and to marvel at the way the sun shines on the windowsill. To love and forgive our flabby stomachs, our pimples and wrinkles, our impatient employers, and our whiny children. To see our loved ones as miracles, our days as gifts, our circumstances as opportunities. To look at pumpkins and see possibilities. To stop waiting for the guy with the glass slipper. To rejoice in what we have today.

Isn't contentment worth far more than a glass slipper? Can't we really be, then, as rich as any princess with a kingdom all her own?

Contentment is a rare treasure. It is, as Paul said, a secret that has to be learned. And the first lesson is that contentment does not equal happiness. Paul didn't say that he was always happy. Many times he was in pain. Many times he was afraid and frustrated. Happiness is a feeling based on our circumstances, but the circumstances of Paul's life were hard. In fact, most of us arrange our days to avoid the level of discomfort Paul suffered. This is a shame, because as long as we pursue happiness, we will most likely not know contentment.

Contentment is an assurance based on the One who is greater than our circumstances. It is born out of suffering and loneliness, having much and then having little, and finding that God is the same and is always sufficient. Happiness is conditioned upon fulfilling our hopes and dreams; contentment comes from knowing Christ. There is nothing wrong with hopes and dreams, unless they become the goal. Claire was right: contentment requires surrender. Until we lay our hopes and dreams at the feet of Christ, we really have very little hope of knowing what will truly fulfill us.

Paul, writing to the new believers in Ephesus, prayed that the eyes of their hearts would be opened, so they could see exactly what God was calling them to do. "Grasp the immensity of this glorious way of life he has for Christians, oh, the utter extravagance of his work in us who trust him!" (Eph. 1:18–20, *The Message*) This is our prayer for you, dear dreamer.

Do you trust Him? Then come with us on our journey. Open your heart, unplug the phone, lock the bathroom door or the office door if you have to, but come with us. Pray with us. Ask God to show you how rich you are, what treasures you have in whatever state you find yourself. Grasp the immensity of this glorious way of life He has for Christians, the utter extravagance of His work in us. God has the power to surpass your dreams. Ask Him to teach you what Paul and Cinderella knew:

Wherever you are, whatever you are doing, there is a reason you can sing.

I have learned to be content whatever the circumstances.
I know what it is to be in need, and I know what it is to have plenty.
I have learned the secret of being content in any and every situation,
whether well-fed or hungry, whether living in plenty or in want.
I can do everything through him who gives me strength.

Philippians 4:11–13

Lord, teach me to adopt Paul's attitude —
to be content in whatever circumstances
I find myself, because I know and trust You.

Lead me to surrender my fantasies,
my castles in the air.
Show me what is good about my life,
and give me a thankful heart.

Lord, give me a song, and
help me to sing for Your glory.

Amen

WHAT ARE
YOUR CIRCUMSTANCES?

As we begin our journey together, jot down some thoughts in response to these questions:

1. What did I previously expect for my life (my hopes and dreams)?

2. What do I still hope for?

3. What circumstances in my life are reasons to rejoice?

2

MOVING TO DISNEY WORLD IS NOT AN OPTION

Claire's chapter about signing a peace treaty with reality

The greatest gift you can give yourself is the gift of reality—the determination to live within the real world, courageously facing each problem with the will to overcome it and not run away.

The more directly you confront the givens of life, the happier you will ultimately be.

Passiveness and helplessness always lead to despair. It is my prayer for you that you will come to love reality.

—Archibald Hart

I will never forget my first visit to Disney World—that wonderful place where reality is temporarily suspended and everything seems possible. For me, it felt very much like coming home. I kept thinking to myself, *This is where I belong—it's where I've always belonged.*

I gasped when I first glimpsed the shimmering towers of Cinderella's castle rising before me. Starry-eyed, I turned to my husband, Spike, and said, "Oh, it's so beautiful. I just wish we could live right here in Fantasyland."

Spike didn't miss a beat.

"Claire," he said gently, "You've been living in fantasyland ever since I met you."

Spike has this amazing way of bringing me right back down to earth. And, okay, I need someone in my life to do that, because dealing with life realistically has never been my strong suit. I would describe my general approach to life as "whimsical" rather than "practical"—as "imaginative" rather than "down-to-earth." (Other people who have had the pleasure of living with me might be more inclined to call me "clueless" or even "out to lunch.")

Reality, in all of its blacks and whites, has always been a struggle for me. I mean, it's just so...so real. But unfortunately, as I have had to learn, there are no "for sale" signs on the colorful streets of Disney World; nobody is moving in on a permanent basis. At some point, every one of its visitors packs up, heads home, and settles down to something called *real life*.

Real life means "what is"—not what we had envisioned or hoped for. It means leaving the castles in the clouds and climbing down the beanstalk to planet earth. It means making a peace treaty between our expectations and our reality.

And therein lies the rub. For I came to the conclusion a long time ago that discontent is almost always linked to expectations. For most of us, the problem is not what we *get* in life, but what we get that's *different from what we'd expected*.

Great Expectations—And Real Outcomes

If we could enter kindergarten or college or marriage or motherhood with absolutely no expectations, we'd probably be spared a lot of grief. Or better yet, if someone could just give us an accurate summary of what to expect from any of the above, we might at least be prepared.

Instead, all too often we find ourselves embarking on our most important life journeys with inaccurate and misleading

road maps. These are maps we've been forced to draw for ourselves, based on such sources as childhood hearsay, cultural
myths, and media hype.

For example, think back on your expectations of romance.
Where did they come from? From books you read? From "girl
talk" at school? From your health education teacher (who
taught the technical facts about male-female relationships,
without ever mentioning the feelings)?

My romantic expectations were shaped by several forces,
most significantly Doris Day movies. In these movies, Doris
behaved in a coy, madcap, and basically airheaded manner for
two solid hours as she subtly but relentlessly pursued Rock
Hudson or some reasonable facsimile of him. She manipulated
like mad, and even lied shamelessly at times. But never mind.
Rock (or whoever) eventually found himself hopelessly smitten
with her anyway, and all ended happily. So what was I to assume?

Other influences that shaped my romantic expectations
were: (1) spying on my sister, Alix, when her boyfriends came
over; (2) listening, fascinated, for hours to my next-door neighbor, Carolyn, who was one year older and purported to know
absolutely everything about boys; and of course (3) the mysterious appearance of certain Ann Landers columns, which I
would find neatly clipped from the daily paper and attached to
my lampshade—articles promising to help the young and
lovelorn avoid a broken heart.

From this motley mixture of advice and innuendo, I
fashioned my expectations of romance. So how closely have
the reality of love and romance matched my youthful
expectations? Go figure.

I also had faulty and inaccurate expectations in other areas
of my life—college, adulthood, and motherhood, to name a

few. And from my personal experience with expectations I have formulated a sort of general-purpose hypothesis that goes something like this: "What we expect in life and what really happens all too rarely intersect."

Random data in support of this hypothesis can be found in almost anybody's life—notably yours and mine. For instance,

We expected a Barbie doll from Aunt Sally for Christmas, and instead we got a Baby Wets-A-Lot.

We expected sunshine the day of the picnic, and instead we got rain (also ants).

We expected Mr. Wonderful to ask us to the prom, and instead we got a call from the president of Nerds Anonymous.

We expected our husbands to be a perfect combination of our fathers and Cary Grant (or Paul Newman or Mel Gibson), and they had the audacity to be themselves.

We expected a glamorous and exciting career, and instead we got eight hours behind a desk and a forty-five-minute commute.

We expected life to be logical, manageable, and somehow "fair." And it turned out to be, at times, about as manageable as a room full of rattlesnakes, and about as logical as an adolescent in love.

Now, there is no possible way for me to see the gulf that lies between your expectations and your reality. Perhaps life has handed you everything you've ever dreamed of on a silver platter. Perhaps you were born beautiful and brilliant and gifted and popular, with just exactly the right size foot to glide gracefully into the glass slipper (which, of course, was held out to you on a satin cushion by a dashingly handsome prince, who vowed his undying affection and has never once swerved from that vow).

But why do I suspect that the previous scenario is not an

accurate description of your life? In the first place, I've never met anyone whose life could be summed up this beautifully. In the second place, would you even have reached for this book if the glass slipper was already comfortably on your foot? I don't think so.

No, I have a hunch that you, like the rest of us, have already had at least some experience with life's occasional habit of dream-dashing and expectation-crunching. (My sister summed it up pretty well after her divorce when she said, "It's not just the man and the marriage I'm grieving for; it's this crazy dream I've always had that everything would turn out happily-ever-after.")

I'm not trying to be morbid or morose. It's just that real lives rarely resemble fairy tales. Even I have managed to learn this. And if you're anywhere past puberty, I have a sneaking suspicion that you've already skinned your knee on reality at least once or twice by now. If you haven't, you will. My mom, who is not only the mother of five, but also a psychologist and something of a sage, puts it this way: "If you're not struggling with something right now, line up! It'll be your turn soon."

Skubalon Happens

So here's another conclusion I have come to after lo, these many years: "Real life" or "reality" is what actually happens while you're waiting around for your expectations to pan out the way you thought they should.

I heard a wonderful sermon once about reality and its total disregard for our expectations. Marshall Craver was the preacher, and his sermon title was "Skubalon Happens." Inspired by a certain tasteless bumper sticker, he had looked up the Greek word for "dung," which he found to be *skubalon.*

His sermon was an inspired message on the redemptive power of God when life's unexpected, unplanned-for unpleasantries conspire to derail our best-laid plans.

Jesus never pulled any punches about "reality." He never set out any false expectations. He told His followers in the clearest possible terms that in this world they would most definitely run head-on into tribulations—trouble, trials, yea, even *skubalon*.

"But be of good cheer," He continued, "I have overcome the world" (John 16:33 NKJV).

Of course, Jesus' ultimate victory over real life on this earth lies in His power to see us through it and finally lift us out of it after death. The reality and quality of eternal existence that we are promised with Him at that point is *Real* in the capital-letter sense. But He made it very clear that His power is for the here and now, also.

So He seems to be saying, "Yes, you do have to live in the real world. And I know that it's no picnic. See, I lived here, too. But don't let it do you in. In Me there *is* a way of overcoming. You can't live in Fantasyland, but you don't have to wallow in the *skubalon,* either!

"Stick with Me. Trust Me, and I'll give you what you need to live victorious lives in the real world."

Welcome to the Real World

But just exactly what do I mean by living in the "real world"? Essentially, living in the real world means coping with the nitty-gritty and the everyday. Waking up. Brushing our teeth. Feeding the dog, the parakeet, the family (whomever). Getting dressed and going about the business of doing whatever it is that we do to exist on planet earth.

And, yes, everybody has to do it.

Reality means going to work, or staying home to work, or not being able to find work. It means paying the bills and cooking a meal and sometimes feeling trapped or lonely or scared or unappreciated.

It means nurturing our relationships, or working hard on difficult relationships, or sometimes being forced to watch a treasured relationship die, however hard we may have tried to save it. It means allowing the persons we love to make their own choices and mistakes, just as we must make our own.

It means using every scrap of our grit, our wit, and our God-given imagination to make the very best we can out of the actual-fact existence we've been given—good days, bad days, and in-between days.

And living in reality, coping with real life in the real world, is one of the biggest challenges of being human. The extent to which we are able to pull it off with some measure of serenity, grace, and purpose will to a great degree determine the quality of our existence.

As I see it, there are three main ways most people deal with the downside of reality. Each has its place, but each falls short as a full-time strategy for handling life. Take it from me, I know. I've tried every one of them!

Strategy #1:
"Don't Look at It, and Maybe It Will Go Away"

Denial has become a popular buzzword for our generation, primarily because so many of us are into it. I, myself, have spent a considerable amount of time there. During my seasons in denial, I have learned what it is and what it is not. And as the now-cliché t-shirt so cleverly has it: "Denial is not a river in Egypt."

Denial means, essentially, in the words of the old musical,

"closing your eyes to a situation you do not wish to acknowl-
edge." It's a trick your mind can pull off when you really don't
want to face some aspect of reality. It simply arranges your
blinders so you won't have to look at it. The reality is there,
but you just can't see it.

Denial, in its place, is appropriate. It is said to be one of the
initial stages of grief, and an indispensable step on the journey
to wholeness after a loss. It gives you time to absorb gradually
the impact of the loss.

Denial in response to loss is similar to what happens when
the body goes into shock after a trauma. Normal physical func-
tions slow down temporarily in order to give the body time to
recover its equilibrium. It's the body's way of shutting down so
that we won't bleed to death or go into a total panic. But if a
person remains in shock without being "brought back," the
shock itself can prove harmful, even fatal.

I experienced some healthy and appropriate denial during
the time that I grieved the death of Spike's mother, Marjorie,
who was my close friend. It took me more than a year after her
death to absorb the fact that she was actually gone. Over and
over I would pick up the phone to call her, or I'd remind
myself to tell her something funny that had happened. Only
gradually did my mind adjust to the reality that she was gone.

Short of developing a psychosis, however, there was no way
I could *permanently* deny the reality of Marjorie's death. Even
though, deep inside, I had somehow expected that she would
always be there for me, I eventually had to come out of that
stage of denial and finally face the reality that she was not.

Although denial (like shock) can be beneficial under certain
circumstances, refusing to let go of our denial can be very
unhealthy and even deadly. The storm we refuse to prepare for

can sink our ship. The physical symptoms we choose to ignore can become a full-blown, incurable disease. The rift in a relationship can become a crack, then a canyon, and finally a divorce. Clinging blindly and stubbornly to our expectations and refusing to see the reality of what is really happening cuts us off from the truth and its power to free us.

Mae West, the early film star, had one of the most classic cases of denial I've ever heard of. She was very beautiful and glamorous in her younger days, and I suppose she expected that her glamour would never fade. As the inevitable wrinkles and lines began to mar her famous face, it is said that Mae West had all of the mirrors removed from her home. If she didn't have to look into the face of reality, she could live on in the land of her unreality.

My great-uncle Ferdinand, too, was a man of stubborn expectations undergirded by denial, or so the family story goes. Ferdinand was the patriarch of a large Roman Catholic family, and it was his heart's desire that at least one of his sons would go into the priesthood.

Of each son, as he came along, Uncle Ferdinand would say in his French accent, "Wonderful boy! Bright as a silver dollar! He's going to be a priest!" None of his sons, however, was even remotely interested in going into the ministry, and none of them ever did.

I can't help but wonder how much time my great-uncle wasted in clinging to his expectations rather than getting to know his boys' own real hopes and ambitions.

Like Uncle Ferdinand, I had expectations for my own two boys. I don't remember specifically putting them into words, but I'm sure my children heard and "felt" those expectations a million different ways. I expected my children to do well and to live up to their academic potential. I expected them to grow up to be nice, polite people and to fit easily into our lives.

Some of my most dramatic lessons in getting past denial have been coming to understand that children arrive with their own personalities and styles of doing things. They come with their own temperaments and quickly develop their own agendas. And they don't always fit in with what we had in mind.

Both of our sons are total originals! Curt, our older son, from earliest childhood was very verbal and inquisitive, with a thoroughly unique way of viewing life. He took nothing for granted and questioned everything.

But it was our younger son Andy's impulsiveness and risk-taking that set me on a journey of deadly denial. What had been adventuresome and mischievous behavior in Andy's grade-school years became dangerous and destructive by the time he was in high school. Gradually, between grades nine and ten, Andy's grades dropped, his friendships changed, and his attitude toward us and everything else in his life became unrecognizable. Every warning sign possible for teenage alcohol and drug abuse was staring me in the face, and yet I didn't see what was happening.

The fact is, I wouldn't see it. I couldn't. Everything in me was working overtime to tell me that Andy's behavior did not indicate what I secretly feared. And because I lived in this state of denial for months and years, our family got sicker instead of healthier, and we almost lost our son.

The good news is that I did get better. Our whole family did. But this improvement was not an overnight process. On my way to getting better, I moved from a state of denying that the problem existed to another way of dealing with reality. I moved into the "fix it" mode.

Strategy #2: "If It's Broke, Fix It!"

The fix-it mode has much to recommend it as a means of dealing with real life problems. A lot of things *can* be fixed, helped, polished, and generally improved by our own efforts. Nothing makes us feel better than to fix something.

My mom, in her practice of psychology, often counsels with people who feel that their lives are totally out of control. And sometimes she gives a simple and surprising initial assignment to these "chaotic" types: "Clean up your car!" She actually sends them off, instructing them not to return until they have done a really super job on the interior and exterior of their automobiles—dejunking, washing, polishing, the works! It's surprising how often these people will come back thoroughly revived and ready to take on the rest of their problems after having had that one small success at getting something in shape.

But there's a problem with the fix-it approach: it can become an addictive way of life. People can get stuck there. And I should know.

People who get stuck in the fix-it mode are sometimes called "fixers." They are people who shop in the "self-help" section of their local bookstores. I know this, too, because I see them there.

Which reminds me of a long-ago incident that tipped me off to my own fix-it addiction. One of our favorite baby-sitters back in the days when our children were small was a delightful, sandy-haired teen named Andolyn. Andolyn possessed the refreshing but sometimes unsettling ability to assess a situation and "tell it like it is."

One evening after getting our boys to bed, Andolyn decided to browse through my bedroom bookshelf. There she discovered my secret passion for self-help books!

"Mama," she told her mother (who is my friend) the next day, "either Mrs. Cloninger knows a whole lot about how to do almost everything, or she is in big trouble!"

In my private stash of reading materials, Andolyn had discovered how-to books on every subject from decorating to dieting, from résumé writing to river rafting. Digging through the stacks, she also found archeological evidence of my pop psychology days, including books that encouraged me to be my own best friend, to pull my own strings, and to treat my psyche cybernetically.

If there were a twelve-step recovery program for "fixers," I would long ago have had to confess to the group, "My name is Claire, and I am a recovering self-help junkie!"

The problem with being a self-help-addicted fixer is not immediately apparent to the fixer herself because, like other addictions, this problem intensifies gradually. We have one small success, and we think we can fix anything and everything. We start with automobile interiors, and the next thing we know we are trying to overhaul our bosses, our husbands, our children, and the entire membership of our churches. We change a tire or a hairdo or the wallpaper in the breakfast room, and the next thing we know we wrongly assume that we also have the power to change and control any and all of those "real life" circumstances that ooze outside the boundaries of our expectations.

The key lesson in the life of any fixer is learning what can be fixed by our efforts and what cannot, what can be remodeled or redone by our own sweat and imagination, and what must be accepted. It is learning what part prayer and faith can play in making changes, and at what point we have stopped praying to God and started nagging Him, stopped seeking God's will and started trying to bully Him into doing our will.

Unfortunately, I had to learn these lessons the hard way—by doing everything wrong. As the cloud of denial lifted, and I finally began to face the fact that our son was struggling with an alcohol and drug problem, I moved directly from denial into my fix-it mode. I unconsciously assumed total responsibility for Andy's problem. I thought if I could just pray a little harder, love him a little more fervently, be a little bit better mother, I could lift him out of the deep and dangerous pit he had dug for himself.

And I tried. Oh, how I tried. I stayed up late into the night typing his term papers. I got him tutors and counselors. I coaxed him and reasoned with him. I lectured him and lied for him. I wore myself out. I worried and paced and prayed myself into a state of exhausted insanity. My prayers were everything but faithful petitions; I was threatening and whining and begging and nagging before the throne of grace.

"God, make him change. You've got to make him change," I kept praying. And it wasn't happening. It was as though my efforts to save Andy were driving the nails into his coffin. The harder I worked on his problem, the less he worked on it. As long as I was staying up nights trying to fix his life, he could get a good night's sleep and wake up rested and ready to rebel a little more the next day.

This was when a friend in my neighborhood (I'll call her Jane) began to share her experience, strength, and hope with me. Jane had gone through a similar problem with her own son, and he had begun to recover only when she had become willing to lovingly let go of him and his problem. When her son could see that she was no longer trying to fix him, he became willing to start dealing with his own problems.

The Lord showed me through my friend's life that there was

only one person I could change—myself. And the only change that would do any good was to let go. I had to stop trying to be God in Andy's life and let God do His job. I had to stop focusing all of my energy on Andy and begin to deal with my own problems. Only in this way would he ever own his problem and begin to deal with it.

God used this very painful experience to teach me one of my life's most important lessons: I cannot fix or change other people. Not even if I feel that I know what is best for them. Not even if I see them destroying themselves and I feel that they must be stopped. Not even if I love them desperately and "only want to help." I cannot fix other people. To try to do so is to thwart the other person's growth—emotionally and spiritually.

God has given each of us free will, and each of us must learn to use it, even if this involves making a lot of wrong choices. To try to fix another person is to get in God's way by trying to do the job that only God can do.

Also, one of the quickest ways to destroy my relationship with someone I love is to try to fix him or her. I can set some healthy boundaries. I can pray and love and encourage. But I cannot fix anyone else.

When a fixer is finally ready to stop fixing, she's ready to get well. When a fixer is finally ready to stop trying to be God, she is ready to move to the next method of dealing with reality—acceptance.

Strategy #3: *"That's the Way It Is"*

I realize that acceptance is not the total answer. Obviously, accepting anything and everything would be foolish and fatalistic. It would leave us with no hope and preempt our faith.

But learning to recognize and accept the things we cannot

change is one of the most vital steps to be taken in dealing with real life and its dilemmas. This kind of acceptance is a power position because it finally puts us in touch with things as they are. It puts us in touch with, and helps us make peace with, the truth. And as the Bible says, the truth will set us free!

I remember reading the testimony of a woman named Karen, and her struggle to accept herself. Karen had been overweight since her teens, and she hated her body. She also blamed and shamed herself over and over for her inability to change her eating habits and lose weight.

Every winter, Karen would determine to lose weight before the next summer. How she longed to lie on the beach, which was only a few miles from her hometown. How she longed to walk in the surf and feel the wind in her hair, the way she had as a child. Every year she would begin by taking off twenty pounds (about half of what she needed to lose). But every year, by the time summer arrived, she had begun to put it on again.

One summer day, as she looked in the mirror and faced her failure once more, Karen realized how much she hated herself. She realized, too, that by clinging to her self-hatred, she was actually giving herself a prison sentence.

"You may not go to the beach until you are perfect, Karen," she was telling herself. As she realized the cruelty and rejection she held in her heart toward herself, Karen wept.

"Would I lock up any other overweight person and forbid her to go to the beach?" she asked herself. She knew that she would not. She would love and encourage anyone else in her position. But instead of showing that kind of love and encouragement to herself, she had become her very own "wicked stepmother," condemning herself to a sad and isolated life.

"Father, forgive me," Karen prayed. "Forgive me for my cruelty to myself. You love me even though I am overweight. You look at me and give me kindness and forgiveness and grace and encouragement. But I have been giving myself only condemnation and cruelty. Help me, Father, to accept and love myself as I am."

An overwhelming tenderness filled Karen's heart at that moment. She knew that what she was experiencing was the tender love of her heavenly Father. She stood before the mirror and looked at herself. What she saw there was a lovely, dark-haired, gentle, overweight woman, with tears streaming down her face, who had not been to the beach in twenty-two years!

At that moment, Karen determined to begin accepting herself. She decided to be on her own side instead of always being her own worst enemy. Karen went shopping that weekend and bought a black swimsuit with hot-pink stripes, a matching beach coat, and hot-pink flip-flops. Then, on impulse, she went into the children's department and bought a plastic bucket and shovel. Now she was ready!

That very afternoon, Karen drove to the beach alone. She kept reminding herself of God's love and acceptance. As Karen stepped into the sand and kicked off her new flip-flops, she experienced once again that childhood pleasure of feeling the sand between her toes.

Karen looked into the faces of the people as she walked by them down the beach. At one time she would have imagined that they were sneering or laughing cruelly at her. Now she knew that the cruel laughter had been in her mind. The people walking by simply saw an overweight woman in a large-size black bathing suit who was obviously taking pleasure in the sunshine and the waves.

An irony of accepting an unpleasant "reality" in our lives is that this acceptance itself often opens a door to change. It was only when Karen was willing to accept and love herself as she was, extra pounds and all, that she was finally able to begin changing her behavior and appearance.

A Gradual Healing

As I accepted the reality of Andy's addiction and let go of the idea that I could fix him, I began to find a new level of peace in my own life. Though the situation did not improve right away, I began to see the dynamics of our family system in a way that I had never seen them before. Like the little child in "The Emperor's New Clothes," I could see what was what! All of us (my husband Spike, our son Curt, and I) had developed unhealthy coping mechanisms to deal with the disruption Andy was causing in the family. Spike had outbursts of anger. Curt, who was attending college in another state, became quiet and withdrawn while he was at home. And I still found myself at times revisiting my old patterns of denial and trying to "fix it."

But with the help of a counselor, we began to look away from Andy and toward ourselves. We began to concentrate on what we could do something about: our own problems. And soon, though Andy was getting worse, we began to get better. We began to pull together as a family. We began to talk more and really listen to one another. And we began to have hope.

Something else changed, too. Spike and I began to pray in a new way: that God would bring some consequences to Andy's behavior that would create a crisis in his life and show him his need for help. This was a scary prayer to pray, but we knew that our son would never ask for or accept help until he could see his need for it.

Our prayers were answered one August night shortly after Andy's graduation from high school. He was arrested and jailed when buying liquor with a forged driver's license. Because he had made the license himself, the charge was forgery—a second-degree felony offense. At one time, this would have seemed like a tremendous tragedy. But Spike and I immediately recognized it as God's hand in our situation, and praised Him for these "consequences."

We decided not to rush right in to rescue Andy when he called, as we once might have done. Instead we let him spend the night in a crowded, depressing cell of the Mobile City Jail, locked in with five other drug offenders. During that long, sobering night, Andy sensed God "knocking on his door."

Since the policeman who had arrested Andy did not show up at his arraignment, the charges were dropped. Andy was able to attend a Christian mountain-climbing camp that had been on the calendar for many months. There on a mountaintop under the blue California sky, Andy gave his life to the Lord. He came home from that trip with a new faith and a new determination to change, with God's help. It was Andy's own decision to enter a ten-week rehabilitation program where he could learn some skills for sober living.

Peace Between "What You Wanted" and "What You Got"

Andy was not the only one who learned a lot during his time in rehab. Spike and I drove over to the treatment center every Saturday to watch films and listen to lectures on this disease of addiction. Curt took a week off from college to go through "family week" with us.

It was during this challenging time that we discovered the

power of praying the well-known Serenity Prayer. We found it
to be a prayer that leads us out of denial, past the fix-it urge,
and beyond fatalistic acceptance. It helps us see things realistically, thereby allowing us to determine the difference between
what we can fix and what we must accept.

During the difficult, exhausting, amazing, miracle-filled
weeks that Andy was in treatment, I learned to pray this
famous prayer with a whole new sense of understanding. Every
day I would pray it in this way:

*God, grant me the serenity to accept the things I cannot
change...* I cannot change Andy or his addiction. I cannot make
him live sober or walk with the Lord. I cannot control the situations that he will encounter when he gets out of treatment. I
cannot single-handedly overhaul this culture in which we live—
a culture that offers dangerous, life-threatening options to our
children. Grant me the serenity to accept the things I cannot
change.

Grant me the courage to change the things I can change...
Lord, I am the only person I can change. I can learn to trust
and love and let go of my fear. I can learn to encourage others
without demanding that they be what I think they should be. I
can work on my own problems and weaknesses and hang-ups.
I can pray with real power and faith and release and abandon,
surrendering my worry to Your strength. I can share my experience, strength, and hope with other parents who are going
through what I went through. I can make my home a place of
welcome and refuge for my family. Grant me the courage to
make these changes.

*And, Lord, grant me the wisdom to know the difference
between the things that I must accept and the things that I can
change. This kind of wisdom can come only from You. Amen.*

Real life in the real world is a tough, nitty-gritty journey that every pilgrim on planet earth must make. Moving to Disney World is not an option. There will be tribulation; Jesus said so. But be of good cheer: He's still in the business of guiding and strengthening and healing and overcoming. And there really is serenity for the asking, right in the middle of it all. And in the end, Real Life with Him forever.

A Postscript

The story I have just shared happened ten years ago. So much has changed since that time. Both of our sons are grown men, grounded in a strong Christian faith. Andy has been gratefully sober (one day at a time) for ten years. He finished college and married a beautiful Christian girl named Jenni. They have two precious children—a girl named Kaylee and a boy named Drew. For four years Andy worked as youth pastor at our church, and now uses his gifts in singing and song-writing to impact young people for Christ. Curt and his wonderful wife, Julie, are the proud parents of little Caroline. Curt loves his job as Website Coordinator for Integrity Music. He also loves leading worship at his church. This year Curt and I wrote a book together entitled *E-Mail from God for Teens*.

As I read the story above, I'm again overwhelmed by God's faithfulness and mercy. I'm overwhelmed by His redemptive and restoring work in our lives. His power is greater than our problems. His grace is greater than our sins. His plan for us far exceeds anything we could ask or imagine.

Sometimes in the darkness of the tunnel it is hard to believe that there is light on the other side. I pray for you now, that you will hold on to and trust God in the midst of your own "real life" challenges. God is not surprised by anything that is going on. He is on the job, working all things together for good. My prayer for you is that our gracious Father will help you to accept the unchangeable things, will help you to change what can be changed, and will grant you the wisdom to know the difference.

Now listen, you who say,
"Today or tomorrow we will go
to this or that city, spend a year there,
carry on business and make money."
Why, you do not even know what will happen tomorrow.
What is your life?
You are a mist that appears for a little while
and then vanishes."

James 4:13–14

No eye has seen,
no ear has heard,
no mind has conceived
what God has prepared for those who love him.

1 Corinthians 2:9

Lord, thank You for the reality of my life—
just as it is today.

Thank You for the grace and the guidance You've given me to
go through what I've been through already.

Lord, I know I've let You and myself and other people down
at times.

Forgive me. Grant me a new perspective on my life . . .
a new beginning.

And even as I am learning to live with joy in this
one moment, give me a glimpse of the beautiful things
You hold in store for me in this life
and in Your ultimate kingdom of Reality.

Help me learn, by Your grace, to live my life today
with joy and celebration for who I am in You.

Amen

EMBRACE REAL LIFE

Think of one major aspect of your life in which reality has fallen outside the boundaries of your expectations. Describe it in writing.

Are you still struggling with this problem? Ask God to give you His insight into it. Then using Claire's version of the Serenity Prayer as a model, write out your present understanding of what can be changed and what must be accepted in your situation.
(Be specific!)

Ask God for His peace and for courage and wisdom to do what must be done.

Go to lunch or coffee with your closest friend, and share your insights and prayers with her.

3

MIRROR, MIRROR ON THE WALL

Karla's chapter about not being an Ideal Woman
(but not being an ugly stepsister, either)

*How beautiful the feet
that bring the sound of
good news and the
love of the King.
How beautiful the
hands that serve
the wine and the
bread and the
sons of the earth.
How beautiful!
How beautiful!
How beautiful is the
body of Christ.*

—Twila Paris

I remember it as if it were yesterday. I was at a Wal-Mart, shopping for flip-flops, pool toys, and sunscreen. I stopped to look at the swimsuit cover-ups, and the entire fashion industry insulted me, right to my face.

There, hanging on a rack in the women's clothing aisle, was a white t-shirt cover-up, looking perfectly harmless. Until I read the tag: *One Size Fits Most.*

Most? One size fits *most?* To me, it was quite obvious what they were saying: *"MOST people would fit into this. How about YOU?"*

Well, maybe it would have fit me, but I'll never know. I was not about to try it on. I walked away and left it hanging there, my silent statement of reproach.

In Quest of the "Ideal Woman"

Why is our self-esteem so tied up in the physical? Maybe yours isn't. But there have been times in my life when I could have flown a spaceship to Mars, become the first woman President, and won a Nobel prize, yet I would have felt like a failure if my skirt wouldn't zip.

I've been on just about every diet available. I've tried the all-protein diet, the all-carbohydrate diet, the all-fruit diet. I've tried eating nothing at all. I've jogged, walked, aerobicized, jazz-danced, low-impacted, and kick-boxed. Four different sizes of clothes hang in my closet, each representing a different stage of success or failure in my efforts to live up to the "Ideal." And just what *is* the Ideal? There is a multi-mega-million-dollar fashion industry out there devoted to promoting it. It shapes our image of the Ideal body, the Ideal clothes, the Ideal hair, the Ideal face. The Ideal Woman never ages. She has ten perfectly manicured nails, the sleek figure of a sixteen-year-old, hair that never frizzes or goes limp, lipstick that stays glossy and unsmudged, and lashes that never clump or flake. She looks equally alluring in her satin teddy as she does in her executive suit. She never has that "not-so-fresh" feeling. And she is oh, so definitely "worth it." I would hate her if she lived next door, but I must confess that more than once I have tried to become her.

I have never succeeded.

The reality is, I've had three children...and my stomach never was flat, even before this. (Isn't that the whole point of pregnancy? For nine whole months we don't have to hold our stomachs in!) I inherited my mother's Horrible Hair, which has the consistency of a broom (no offense, Mom). I'm starting to get wrinkles and age spots. (I think that if you have those, you should be exempt from having pimples anymore. Fair is fair.)

I despair of ever being ideal. I know there are some ideal women out there, because I run into one every now and then at the mall. (Of course, she's shopping in a different department than I!) I look at her, and I do *not* think, "Wow, she must be exhausted." But in fact, she really must be. It takes a lot of work to be ideal. It's a constant vigil, a perpetual battle against split nails, dry skin, graying hair, and that great enemy of the ideal woman: cellulite.

Know why it's so much effort to be ideal? Because Ideal is Not Real.

The Me I See

In his book *The Challenge of the Disciplined Life: Christian Reflections on Money, Sex & Power,* Richard Foster writes that the reason pornography is so destructive is that it corrupts our ability to appreciate reality. No average housewife, reasons Foster, can compete with an airbrushed centerfold. The centerfold is fantasy; nobody really looks like that. But the more time a man spends with this fantasy, the less reality appeals to him.

In a subtle way, the fashion industry has offered us its own version of pornography: slim, sleek bodies of eighteen-year-olds made up to look thirty. This, we have been told, is the Ideal. This is how a woman should look. But this high-fashion ideal is just as much a fantasy as the centerfold; most us will never look like that. In fact, models say it takes hours of makeup and hair-styling, and a lifetime of rigorous diet and exercise for them to look like that. Most of us have fifteen minutes to put on our makeup; we don't have personal trainers or people to follow us around with special lighting. So what's our realistic hope of ever measuring up?

Our culture is doing a number on us, and it's hard to escape. Psychologists tell us that until girls reach the age of ten or eleven, they are fairly self-confident and have a positive body image. But by the time they are only two years older, they will have developed a negative body image and will become awkward and unsure of themselves. More than ninety percent— *ninety percent!*—of American women have a negative body image and consider themselves to be lacking in some area of their appearance.

My "body image" is not what I see in the mirror. It is what I see in my head; it is my mind's picture of how I look. An amazing phenomenon has been discovered in many weight-loss clinics. When a client loses pounds and pounds of weight, she often still envisions herself as a fat person, and consequently responds to the world from this point of view.

I have a friend who experienced this kind of distorted body image—not with her weight, but with the size of her nose. Jean had a perfectly good nose, as far as I could see, but to her it was huge. Like the man in the sinus spray commercial, when Jean looked in the mirror she saw nothing but a big nose protruding. So she had reconstructive surgery—a "nose job." Jean confesses to me that she is still surprised every time she looks in the mirror and sees her tiny, perfect nose. Her mind still carries the image of the old, "big" one.

I cannot remember a time in my life when I have felt confident about my body. Even as far back as the age of twelve and thirteen, I dreaded the arrival of summer—the season of shorts and swimsuits. I was too fat, my stomach pooched, my hips were too wide. My friends looked great. I looked awful.

As I write this, I get out my old picture albums and look through snapshots of me with Nancy Lewis at her family's lake cabin. There we are, smiling on the dock with our beach towels and our bottles of Sun-In. And I am surprised to see not just one skinny, knobby-kneed girl in a bikini (Nancy)—but two! Where did I ever get the idea that I was fat?

I'll tell you where. I got it by doing what every other American teenage girl was doing in the summer of 1969. I was poring over pictures of Cheryl Tiegs smiling out at me from the pages of *Seventeen* magazine, and I was comparing myself. I let the media whisper its fantasies to me, and the reality I saw in the mirror couldn't compare. I was thirteen; my body hadn't even developed yet, and I'd already decided that my body wasn't good enough.

I'm much older now—and so is Cheryl Tiegs, but she still looks better than I do. Lauren Hutton is almost as old as my mother, and she looks better than I do! (Sean Connery is . . . what? . . . a hundred years old, and he looks better than I do!) I'm still comparing myself. I may be older, but I'm not much wiser.

Why do I have such a hard time affirming my body? I love my husband's body. I love the shape of it, the smell of it, the familiarity of it. I love my children's bodies. I love Seth's long, lanky legs, Matt's almond-shaped eyes, and Ben's sturdy little torso. I love the feel of their skin; I marvel at their individual beauty. Why can't I marvel at myself? Why can't you?

Because our standard is skewed. The magazines have lied to us. We are victims of pornography. We have looked at the glossy pictures so long that looking in the mirror is painful.

Looking at the Truth

The Bible doesn't tell us what Jesus looked like. This should tip us off as to how important looks are to God! What we do know is what Jesus did with the body He was given: He touched, He healed, He spoke the truth, He fed the hungry, He bounced children on His knee. He built things skillfully, He caught fish, He ate and drank, laughed and cried. And in the end, He sacrificed His body. The one physical description of Christ we are allowed is of His death on the cross: "His appearance was so disfigured beyond that of any man and his form marred beyond human likeness. . . . He had no beauty or majesty to attract us to him, nothing in his appearance that we should desire him. He was despised and rejected by men, a man of sorrows, and familiar with suffering. Like one from whom men hide their faces he was despised, and we esteemed him not" (Is. 52:14; 53:2–3).

Is it hard to look? Don't turn away. This is what true beauty looks like to God. This is the true Ideal, the One we should pore over and paste on our walls and imitate. This is God's Standard-Bearer, the One in whom God is well-pleased.

Made by Him to Be Like Him

God Himself fashioned our bodies. I love James Weldon Johnson's description of God, "like a Mammy bending over her baby," toiling with a piece of clay to make us just right. This creation is more intricate, more detailed than all the others, because this one is a tiny model of the Creator Himself. He gave us hands so that we can be craftsmen, like our Maker. He added strong arms and legs to lift, carry, build, climb, run, hunt, jump; intricate brains to think and communicate, respond to our world and to Him; emotions so that we can feel and know and love, as we are known and loved by the One who made us. He gave us bodies that can nurture and protect; help and heal; change and age; and understand and celebrate our Creator as we come to understand and celebrate ourselves.

There is no joy, no beauty, no celebration in preserving ourselves, carefully keeping ourselves back, to be ornamental and cold upon shelves. There *is* joy in being used, in becoming vessels, broken to spill out the fragrance of Christ on everyone we touch. There is beauty in dying—dying to adolescence and becoming young women, dying through childbirth to bring forth new life, dying to youth and finding a new age, dying to vanity and discovering that true beauty is far more glorious than looking good. True beauty is looking like Christ.

Jesus was not afraid to be mussed or sullied. He didn't worry about sweating or getting dirty or getting wrinkles. He was a King, but nobody waited on Him; in fact, He waited on others. He washed feet. He served meals. He gave us an example: "This is my body, broken for you" (Luke 22:19).

Robert Benson has a touching view of our being like Christ, even in His brokenness. "To take [communion with Him] is to enter into the fourfold pattern—taken, blessed, broken, shared—that not only forms the core of the great prayer but forms the core of the life of the Spirit itself.I have always enjoyed the part of the prayer that suggests to us that we are taken by God, that we are chosen....I am happy, too, to think about being blessed by God as well....And I particularly enjoy the part about being shared....It is the broken part that I do not care for very much. It is the broken part, however, that makes everything else...The lesson is that Jesus of Nazareth— the most chosen and most blessed and most shared one of us all—was the most broken of us all.

"If the Christ is to be seen in this world now, then what happened to the Christ must happen to us. . . . We, too, must be taken, blessed, broken, and shared."[1]

Our physical bodies—however lumpy, short-limbed, skinny, or pale—are Christ's tools for doing His work in this world. My pastor, Mike Glenn, often closes our service by reminding us, "If God goes anywhere this week, it will be our feet that carry Him. If God says anything to anyone, it will be with our mouths. If God touches anyone, it will be with our hands. And if He loves anyone, it will be with our hearts. We are the Body of Christ."

As Christ's body, I can do some wonderful things. I can touch. I can hug. I can give a drink of water. I can bandage a skinned knee. I can laugh and splash in the creek. I can yell my head off at a soccer game, or silently speak volumes as I look into the eyes of one I love. I can bathe and dress an aging parent or rock a baby. I can share the pain of a friend's disappointment, celebrate her victory, listen to her confidences. I can plant a neighbor's garden, roof a Habitat house, tutor an inner-city mother, tell a Bible story to a Backyard Bible Club, play basketball with students in Poland, administer first aid to villagers in Costa Rica. I can scrub toilets and I can sing praises. I can make sandwiches and I can send emails. I can sit in Congress and I can sit by a bedside. I can run for office, and I can run to the grocery store. I can run a marathon. I can stand up for truth, and I can kneel in prayer on behalf of the whole world. I am fearfully and wonderfully made!

So are you. Short or tall, skinny or not so skinny, single or married, young or old—your body is more than just a pair of breasts, a womb, a flat stomach, or a great complexion. Your particular combination of arms, ears, eyes, hands, feet, heart—

combined with your own set of gifts and opportunities—make your experience of being human as unique to you as mine is to me. Contrary to what the media show us and tell us, there is no one standard for femininity. Part of the miracle of being a woman is that each of us, like a snowflake, is a complete and original expression of womanhood. With each new day that goes by, we are constantly changing and expressing, in a new and unique way, what one woman looks like. And if God is at work in us, every day we are coming to reflect more and more what He looks like!

I guess we can be ideal after all. It depends on whose standard we consider the true measure—God's or the world's. "Listen, O daughter, consider and give ear: Forget your people and your father's house. The King is enthralled by your beauty; honor *Him*, for *He* is your Lord" (Ps. 45:10–11, emphasis mine).

Family Resemblance

I have a picture, taken at our family's river cabin, of my mother in her sun hat and old swimsuit, standing with her feet in the cold current. She is not the thinnest person in the picture, nor the youngest. Others have better figures and deeper tans. To me, however, she is the most beautiful. She gazes out at me, a graceful reflection of God's glory. Her sense of self inspires me.

I have other pictures of her in my memory: young and slim, fashionable as Jackie Kennedy in her Easter suit and pillbox hat; tromping through the woods at a Camp Fire Girls retreat; scooping up shells on the beach with her grandsons. I remember how glamorous she seemed, all dressed up for a Saturday night out with Dad; how comforting it was to have her crawl into bed with me when I was scared in the middle of the night.

I remember how I admired her, how I played dress-up with her jewelry and old formals, yearning to grow up and be just like her. And I do have my mother's eyes, her hair, and some of her style. We kind of smile alike. There is a lot in me that comes from her. Family resemblance.

I remember how I felt when I first laid eyes on my own children. I knew they were mine — each of them — because of their little mouths. Each one had a tiny, pink, bird-like mouth, just like my own baby pictures. Their strange little faces somehow looked familiar.

"Wow," I thought, "that's a part of me!" How amazing.

You and I must realize that our bodies also bear a family resemblance — to a heavenly Father who created us in His image, and to an older Brother who showed us how to reflect that image. Our Father labored over each one of us to make us each uniquely like Himself in some way. When we were born, He stepped back and said to Himself, "Wow! Will you look at that . . . that's a part of Me!"

How amazing. How ideal.

[1] Benson, Robert, *Living Prayer* (New York: Jeremy P. Tarcher/Putnam, 1998), 39–40.

For you created my inmost being;
you knit me together in my mother's womb.
I praise you because I am fearfully and wonderfully made;
your works are wonderful, I know that full well.
My frame was not hidden from you when I was made in the
secret place.
When I was woven together in the depths of the earth,
your eyes saw my unformed body.
All the days ordained for me were written in your book
before one of them came to be.

Psalm 139:13–16

Father Creator, forgive me for failing to marvel at Your
handiwork in me.

Thank You for making this amazing body!
Teach me how to love it as You love it.
Train me to care for it and cherish it—
not to make it an idol.

I offer myself to You.
Take my body, mind, and soul.
Use me—all of me—for Your purposes and Your glory.

Show me how my body is a reflection of You,
and free me to celebrate that reflection.

Amen

CELEBRATE YOURSELF

Get out your family albums and spend a few moments
looking back at your heritage. Whose nose did you
inherit? Whose smile? Whose sense of humor?

Look back at how you have changed over the years:
holidays, weddings, graduations, birthdays, babies,
vacations, the fat periods, the skinny periods,
the bad hairdos. You, and only you, have lived these
moments. Thank God for who He has made you to be.

Make a list of your skills, strengths, experience,
and expertise.

Search your community ministries for needs that
match what only you have to offer. Volunteer!

4

A Kiss for the Frog Prince

Claire's chapter about good days, rotten days,
and amazing days.

*We cannot earn or win
anything from God;
we must either receive
it as a gift or do without
it. The greatest blessing
spiritually is the knowl-
edge that we are desti-
tute; until we get there,
our God is powerless.
He can do nothing for
us if we think we are
sufficient of ourselves.
We have to enter into
His Kingdom through
the door of destitution.*

—Oswald Chambers

In my life there are good days and
there are bad days. On a good day, I
can really feel God's love. It's almost
tangible.

On a good day I wake up early. I run
three or four miles. I have a long and
meaningful prayer time. I am in my
office writing by nine o'clock, and I
have wonderful ideas that I translate
into a song or a chapter certain to
change somebody's life for the better. I
eat leafy green and yellow vegetables,
and when offered gooey desserts, I
smile and say, "no thank you." I do not
watch TV. I feel charitable toward the
members of my family and say encouraging things all day long. I am kind to
friends, strangers, and small animals.
In the evening, I cook a meal in which
nothing burns or is underdone. I wash
the dishes and plump the pillows on

the sofa, take a warm bath, and put on a clean nightie. I fall into bed and think, *Of course God loves me. What's not to love? I am a doll!*

But a bad day is a very different story. On a bad day I wake up late and growl even before my eyes are fully open. I figure I've already missed my prayer time, so I scratch that. I am cross with my husband, my neighbors, my friends, salespersons in stores, people in traffic, and innocent children. I gossip about people I should be praying for. I make resolutions to stop doing this, and the next time the phone rings I'm at it again. I watch hours of TV and eat mounds of potato chips. I do not write a word nor move a muscle. By the time I turn out the light at night, there is only one word to describe me: *yuk*.

Not only do I not love myself, but I find it impossible to believe that God, Jesus, or anyone even remotely associated with heaven could locate a kind thought to send my way. I mean, some days it gets severe.

This description of my good and bad days demonstrates something unfortunate and skewed about my expectations of God. I keep expecting Him to act like I do. I keep expecting Him to love like I love. I keep expecting Him to give me what I think I deserve. And, of course, He doesn't.

Only One Speed

What is really true about my good and bad days, as far as God is concerned? On which days would you figure He loves me most, on a scale from one to ten? Actually, as you might guess, it's the same—exactly the same. On a scale from one to ten, God loves me a ten on my best days and a ten on my worst days.

How can He do this? How can He get away with being so indiscriminate? I think it has something to do with the fact that

He's God, and His capacity to love is not dependent in any way on my ability to perform.

Better go over this one more time. It's a biggie. *God's love is not dependent on my performance.* It is not rationed out to me in proportion to my goodness or badness on any given day.

God's capacity to love is linked instead to the fact that His whole nature is totally turned toward love. In fact, He *is* love. He's made of love. He overflows with love. Love is His composition, His content. Love is His definition and His job description. Love is God's occupation and preoccupation. It's His mission and His passion and His favorite pastime. Love is who God is and what He does.

And God's love comes in only one speed: ten. *Ten.* Crank it up. Floorboard it. Pedal to the metal. Full speed ahead. Good days, bad days, and in-between days, it's coming at me. Paid for and free for the asking, full-to-overflowing, broken and poured out. I didn't earn it, I don't deserve it. There's no way I can ever pay it back, and yet it's mine.

What's more, there's no way I can lose God's love by what I do or don't do. And there is no way I can improve it by what I do or don't do. There's nothing I can do to make Him love me less, and nothing I can do to make Him love me more.

Amazing, you say? You bet it is! It is, quite simply, the best-kept secret of the Christian life—the much-discussed but little-understood mystery we call "amazing grace."

What We Deserve and What We Get

I've spent a large part of my Christian journey trying to get a handle on grace. As a child of this performance-oriented culture which gives its rewards to the high achievers and first-place finishers, I must admit that I stand open-mouthed at the very idea of a God who loves me "just because." I am amazed and tongue-tied and more than a little bit uncomfortable to find myself presented with a prize I didn't win, a reward I didn't earn, and an astounding reality I struggle to internalize.

What do I deserve, if not grace? Theologically speaking, I deserve hell—since by God's standard of measurement, anything short of perfection gets a thumbs-down.

Comedian and singer Mark Lowry realized this when he was griping to God about not getting paid what he deserved after a performance. After his griping had died down for a minute, Mark sensed God saying, "Mark, if you got what you deserved, it would be pure hell."

Based on that experience, Tommy Greer and I wrote a tongue-in-cheek song for Mark to use in his concerts. In the lingo of the comedian, it expresses Mark's theological revelation about not getting what we deserve:

When the market's plunging and inflation peaks,
When your in-laws drop in to spend the week,
When the rain keeps pouring through the roof that leaks,
And you don't feel very well;
When your job is throwing you a major curve,
And all your friends begin to work your nerves,
It's mild compared to what you deserve,
'Cause what you deserve is hell!

And it sure beats hell; it sure beats hell!
Considering where you could be now,
you're doing pretty well.
So count your blessings, dude; work up some gratitude;
You know, you could be barbecued,

And it sure beats hell; it sure beats hell.

You could be checking in tonight to Lucifer's motel.

So don't be a thankless slob; Jesus Christ has done the job.

And you're not a shish-kabob;

And that sure beats hell![1]

Playing by the Wrong Rule Book

Don't get me wrong. Even though the idea of grace sometimes makes me feel uncomfortable, considering the alternatives, I'm delighted to receive it!

It's just that sometimes I feel as if I've spent most of my life trying to measure up, to earn and achieve and be good enough. And then suddenly, I am confronted with this incredible Person who loves me anyway—no matter what. And it's a little like being somewhere near the middle of the third quarter and abruptly realizing I've been playing by the wrong rule book all the time! All the yardage I thought I had gained early in the game (by striving to achieve) has done nothing to improve my position. God would have loved me anyway!

I don't think I'm alone in my failure to grasp God's grace. Let's face it. Our culture does little to prepare us for the idea of it. Even those of us from the most nurturing homes have lived under the terms of "conditional love." Parents, teachers, and society in general have let us know that the world likes a good little girl or boy better than the other variety.

Even the most loving parents attach conditions to their approval and rewards—at least some of the time: "You can do this if you'll do that." And because we have had so little experience with the totally unconditional nature of God's love, we often find it baffling.

A Picture of Grace

Victor Hugo's great novel, *Les Miserables,* includes an unforgettable scene in which a man finds himself totally bewildered by an unexpected touch of grace. Jean Valjean, the protagonist, has been released from prison after serving years for merely stealing a loaf of bread. He spends his first night of freedom in the home of kindly old Bishop Myriel. There he's given the first good meal and comfortable bed he has known in years. Valjean, distrustful of the bishop's kindness, thanks his benefactor by stealing his silverware.

When Valjean is captured by the police and returned to the home of the bishop, he naturally expects to be charged with the theft and returned to the hellish existence of life in prison. To his amazement, however, the compassionate Myriel tells the policemen that the silverware had not been stolen at all, but was presented as a gift to Valjean. No charges are pressed.

Then, to heap grace upon grace, Bishop Myriel lifts two heavy silver candlesticks from his mantel and hands them to Valjean, saying, in effect, "Here, Jean, you forgot to take these candlesticks, which I also meant for you to have."

This is a picture of grace. It is kindness we did not expect, and generosity we did not deserve. It is a gift we could never earn from a friend of whom we are not worthy. And when it comes unexpectedly into our lives, if we've been playing the game out of another rule book, it can be difficult to understand and awkward to accept. We stand dumbstruck, fumbling for the proper response.

A Spiritual Dunce Cap

It would seem that after all the grace I've received in my lifetime, I would know by now the proper response. But grace is a lesson I keep having to learn, over and over again.

When I finally decided to let God be in control of my life on a cold January night more than twenty years ago, I understood grace perfectly—and I knew it was exactly what I needed. To begin with, I knew I was out of answers of my own. I knew I was about as needy as I had ever been. It was easy to see myself as a drowning refugee cast in turbulent waters because, spiritually, that's exactly what I was. I was splashing and sputtering and dog-paddling as hard as I could, and still I was slipping under the waves.

It was easy for me to know that I needed a Savior, and I grabbed at the grace God held out to me like a life preserver. But once the Lord had gotten me to shore, had gotten the water out of my lungs, and had dried me off, I thanked Him profusely and said, in effect, "I'm okay now. I'll take it from here. You've done the hard part; now I'll take over. I'm going to live for You now and be a really good person. Not to worry. Leave it to me."

Then, without even realizing it, I went right back to struggling in my own strength—with only one slight alteration. I went from my old routine of dancing for the approval of the world to dancing for the approval of God and His people. I went from my old litany of "shoulds" and "oughts" to a new and sanctified set.

Like the little pig leaving home to make his fortune in the world, I set out to make good in this new kingdom. Since performance had always earned points for me in the old kingdom, I saw no reason to abandon that game plan. So I set out, on some unconscious level, to "perform" spiritually. (I know this sounds silly. It *is* silly. But that's how clueless I was.)

Most mornings, as I entered my prayer time with the Lord,

I felt the pressure of some intangible quota I had to meet. I felt obliged to chalk up a certain number of minutes per day or hours per week, though no one was keeping score but me.

Then there was the "quality gauge" I unconsciously attached to my spiritual experiences. On days when I felt that I had really heard from God, really stated my case well to Him, really enjoyed my time of praise and gotten a lot out of the Bible reading, I felt fantastic. But at other times, when nothing much seemed to have happened, I felt like a failure.

And then there were the mornings when, exhausted from the ongoing demands of children and career, I would get up early for a quiet time with the Lord, and actually fall asleep with my face in the Bible. I'd wake up to find that I had been drooling onto the pages of 2 Chronicles. At times like that I felt certain that Billy Graham, Mother Teresa, and other spiritual giants were sitting on the front row as God's favorites, and that I was in the corner wearing a dunce cap.

A Hundred-Pound Backpack

When I look back at my workaholic determination to earn God's approval, and my inability to understand His grace, I am reminded of the old story of a traveler carrying a hundred-pound backpack.

A road-weary traveler had walked all day carrying a hundred-pound pack on his back. Finally, after many miles, a sturdy, horse-drawn wagon pulled up alongside, and the driver offered the poor traveler a ride. Gratefully accepting the offer, the traveler climbed wearily into the cart and sat beside the driver. But he refused to take the heavy bundle off his back.

"Please, sir," the driver encouraged his passenger, "Won't you put your heavy bundle down? There is ample room in my cart for

it, and I know that your shoulders must be aching from the load."

"Never mind," the traveler replied. "I can carry it. I'm very used to it, you see." And so on he rode, stupidly shouldering the back-breaking load.

Little by little, I am learning to put down my back-breaking load of self-effort and enjoy the ride. Gently, patiently, again and again, God keeps taking me back to the drawing board on the subject of grace. With enormous perseverance and a good sense of humor, He continues my higher education in the class-room of His mercy. And though I am thick-headed and more than a little stubborn, I have gradually come to realize many things.

The Rock in My Pinafore Pocket

One thing I've realized is that I had experienced many touches of grace before I ever tried to understand the term. One of the first grace-filled moments I can remember hap-pened when I was only six.

My first-grade teacher was a lovely, white-haired, grand-motherly woman named Mrs. Sullivan. Her classroom was full of wonderful things. But the best of all was a dazzling rock collection that she kept attractively displayed on the shelves behind her desk.

All of us kids loved that rock collection. Some days, if we finished our desk work ahead of time, we were permitted to walk up and down in front of the shelves, admire the rocks with their different shapes and colors, and try to read the identifying cards with their mysterious names. But we knew the rules. We could look, but we were not to touch!

My favorite rock of all was the most impressive one in the collection. It sparkled with what seemed to be a million different planes and facets. It was crystal clear, with a slightly pinkish cast. It was beautiful.

One spring afternoon, when I had finished my desk work early and was standing alone behind Mrs. Sullivan's desk, admiring my favorite rock, I was suddenly overwhelmed by a desire to pick it up. The next thing I knew, I had put it in the pocket of my pinafore!

My heart pounded like a sledgehammer. I felt like my whole body had a violent case of hiccups! My cheeks burned, and I was terrified at my predicament. I knew I couldn't keep the rock, but I didn't know how to put it back without being noticed.

I walked home that afternoon as I usually did, but I was so upset that when I reached my front door, I threw it open and ran sobbing into my mother's arms.

"I've taken a rock from Mrs. Sullivan's collection," I blurted out tearfully, "and you've gotta go and put it back, Mom."

My mother had a great opportunity for a lecture at this point; but I think she could see that I didn't need to be convinced of my guilt. Instead of scolding, she held me and comforted me, and thanked me for my honest confession. Then in a very gentle voice, she told me that I would have to return the rock myself and apologize to Mrs. Sullivan.

I died a million deaths. I anguished. I pleaded with her to do it for me. But she was already getting the car keys and leading me to the car. Before I knew it, we were on our way back to school. Mom parked the car and walked me as far as the classroom door.

A Little Chip of Grace

I can see that classroom as clearly in my mind's eye today as I saw it that afternoon. The desks were empty, but the overhead lights were still on, and Mrs. Sullivan was at her desk. Slowly I approached the desk, holding the pink crystal rock like a burning coal in my hand.

"Mrs. Sullivan," I almost whispered, as she looked up at me. "I took your rock," I said, holding it out to her and feeling my eyes begin to burn. "I'm sorry," I said…and began to sob.

I was paralyzed, waiting for the verbal abuse I knew I deserved. But it never came. Instead, my teacher did something I will never forget. She put her arms around me and held me close.

"I'm very proud of you, Claire," she said softly. "Returning the rock was the right thing to do, and you did it right away. I'm very proud of you."

What she did next was the most tender and kind thing I could ever have imagined. After all of these years, my heart melts when I remember it. She took me by the hand and told my mother that we would be right back. Then we walked together down the hall to the little supply room, where we found our school janitor, Mr. Pete.

"Mr. Pete," Mrs. Sullivan said, handing him the pink crystal rock, "I want Claire to have a little piece of this rock to keep. Do you think you could chip one off for her?"

"I sure could," he said. And that's exactly what he did.

In some way that I didn't fully understand at the time, that rock became very important to me. It was more than a pretty rock, more than a favorite possession. Holding it was like having, in my hands, a little chip of grace.

Those who dispense grace to others often do more than they know they are doing. I received so much that day. I received a blessing and a lesson from my mother, whose grace that day was not cheap. She forgave me and loved me, but she didn't spare me the pain of owning up to my crime. She loved me enough to make me stand up and do the right thing.

And I received a different kind of blessing from Mrs. Sullivan. She forgave me, too, and affirmed me; but she did more than that. Her grace went beyond forgiveness to mercy. She let me know that I was very important to her. More important, in fact, than the rules I had broken, and more important than her treasured possession, which I had pocketed and gone home with. By her willingness to chip off a part of that pink crystal treasure for me, my teacher was saying, "You mean more to me than anything I own."

Glimpses of Grace

Jesus always saw the importance and affirmed the value of the individual. When others saw a woman caught in adultery, a sinner ripe for stoning, He saw a desperate and wounded soul in need of forgiveness, a potential saint who was capable of higher things. (See John 8:3–11.)

When His disciples would have sent the noisy, dusty crowd of little children away, Jesus stopped everything He was doing. He smiled, opened His arms, and said, "Let them come to Me." And as He picked them up and set them on His knee, everything about Him said, "You matter to Me. You're not a nuisance. You are a treasure." (See Matthew 19:13–15, Mark 10:13–16, and Luke 18:15–17.)

When the parade of life was passing by the little man who had climbed up in a tree, Jesus stopped the parade and called up, "Come down, Zacchaeus. You matter to Me. It's you I want to have supper with tonight." (See Luke 19:1–9.)

When the one they had always shunned and called "maniac" and "demon child" fell foaming and raving at His feet, Jesus saw something that the others could not see. He saw the desperate prisoner inside a mad disguise, a man in need of mercy. And He called that man forth to be calm and clothed in his right mind. (See Matthew 8:28–33, Mark 5:2–6, and Luke 8:27–36.)

Jesus gave grace constantly. When He spoke to demoniacs and prostitutes and beggars, when He ate with tax collectors and sinners, He was saying with His life, "There are no unimportant people. Everyone is valuable to My Father and to Me."

The Language of Grace

The ultimate and definitive word of grace was spoken on Calvary, where Jesus allowed His bruised and tortured body to be nailed to a cross for us. Though all of our choices be unworthy, though all of our efforts fall short, He holds in His heart such a love for us, such a desire to see us reconciled to His Father, that He was willing to go through hell on earth to spare us hell for eternity.

This is the gospel that Brennen Manning has dubbed "the ragamuffin gospel." It is a gospel not for the Pharisee or spiritually muscle-bound, not for the "fearless and the tearless," but a gospel that stoops to embrace the bedraggled, beat-up, and burnt-out...the wobbly and weak-kneed, who know they don't have it all together...the poor, weak, sinful men and women with hereditary faults and limited talents...the earthen vessels who shuffle along on feet of clay...the smart people who know they are stupid and the honest disciples who know they are scalawags.

This is a gospel that reaches down into the heart of your life and my life. This is very good news indeed!

Kissing the Frog

Would it surprise you to know that the "ragamuffin gospel" is the theme of one of my favorite fairy tales? There are no glass slippers in this quaint little parable of grace. It's the story of a toad of a guy who longs for somebody to love him, warts and all. It is called "The Frog Prince."

In "The Frog Prince," a beautiful princess develops an unlikely friendship with a talkative frog who lives in her pond. She grows so fond of him, in fact, that one day she bends down and plants a big kiss on his green and warty lips. Magically, that kiss breaks a wicked spell, and the frog turns into a handsome and charming prince. Of course, you know where the story goes from there. "Happily ever after" is a foregone conclusion.

God's grace comes to us a lot like that kiss. It comes to us exactly as we are, warts and all. And when it does, it totally rewrites our rule books. It tells us that we are loved and prized and very, very worth it, just as we are.

It also tells us that on our best days and on our worst days we are valuable to God, regardless of whether we *feel* valuable. It teaches us to trust God's opinion of us rather than our own feelings about ourselves.

Our feelings are a wonderful, God-given gift, but they were never meant to direct the course of our lives. They are a faulty compass that lead us around and around in circles. They render us unable to navigate outside of our own limited perspective.

God's grace, on the other hand, is the compass we can trust. Like the North Star, it is always true. It keeps us looking up into the amazing and unshakable stellar truths of who we are in Heaven's sight: We're His kids, His creation, His children, His own. And He is certifiably nuts about us!

God's grace frees us from the prison of seeking inner contentment by trying to be good enough. And it releases us into the wonder and joy that Abraham Heschel must have felt when he wrote the words, "Just to be is a blessing. Just to live is holy."

God's grace invites us into an intimate love relationship with the One who died so that we can live. It says, "I no longer call you servants, because a servant does not know his master's business. Instead, I have called you friends" (John 15:15). It opens the door to prayer that is conversation, and praise that is as natural as breathing.

And like the kiss of the princess that transformed the frog, grace transforms us. It transforms our lives of struggling and striving and approval-seeking into lives of sanity and serenity and something worth celebrating.

Even when the glass slipper doesn't fit.

[1]"Sure Beats Hell," lyric by Claire Cloninger, melody by Tommy Greer, © Word Music, 1991. Used by permission.

For it is by grace you have been saved,
through faith—and this not from yourselves,
it is the gift of God—
not by works, so that no one can boast.
For we are God's workmanship, created in
Christ Jesus to do good works,
which God prepared in advance for us to do.

Ephesians 2:8–10

For it is God who is at work within you,
giving you the will and the power
to achieve his purpose.

Philippians 2:13, Phillips

Father, I thank You for giving me not what my sin merits,
but what Your love decrees; not what I expect or deserve,
but what You know I need.

Help me to put down my heavy load of self-effort
and receive the reality of Your unconditional love,
which re-creates me in Your image.

Help me to see Your hand of grace all around me,
in the circumstances and people You bring into my life.

May Your grace in me be contagious, Lord.
May it spread from my life to others around me.

Amen

CELEBRATE GOD'S GRACE

Look back at your life and remember some of your own "rock-in-the-pinafore-pocket" experiences—times you received something good that you did not deserve.

How have these incidents of grace shaped you and made you who you are?

Look at this day as a gift of grace. Take time to appreciate the little, grace-filled moments and activities you tend to take for granted. Enjoy the sunshine, a cup of coffee, a visit with a friend. Thank God all day long for His many "tender mercies." And enjoy the blessing that goes with extending mercy to someone else.

During your prayer time, write God a letter. Thank Him for His grace in your life, beginning with the gracious gift of His Son.

5

BIBBIDY-BOBBIDY-BOO

Karla's chapter about doing it all—and what to do
when it does you in

Every little girl has three dress-up
outfits: princess, bride, and nurse. We
carry these with us into womanhood,
if not in our toy chests, at least in our
hearts. And some of us, secretly, under
our business suits or jeans, wear another
outfit: the red cape and the suit with a
golden S on the chest.

Where did we get the idea that we
have to be Superwoman—able to do it
all with grace and efficiency? Was it
from June Cleaver, in her pearls and
heels, baking cookies for Ward and the
Beave? Or Scarlet O'Hara ("As God is
my witness, I'll never be hungry
again!")? How about Nancy Drew, teen
Superwoman, who could sleuth around
in dusty attics and still dress in time for the dinner dance? Or
Jane Fonda, who proved we could be politically active and

look great in leg warmers? Worst of all was that awful woman in the TV ad who could "bring home the bacon, fry it up in a pan, and never, ever let him forget he's a man"!

Take your pick. Superwoman role models abound.

My First Role Model

I first got the impression that "real women can do it all" from my mother. Because, quite frankly, she *can.*

She cooks (from scratch). She sews (without a pattern). She gardens (from seed). She decorates (without a consultant). She runs a business, does her own hair, volunteers, is well-read, goes out to dinner, still charms my dad, and even hangs her laundry out to dry because "it smells better than the dryer." And of course, she doesn't look her age. For her birthday, Dad gave her a t-shirt that reads, "Still Perfect after All These Years."

It isn't easy to have a mom like that. I tried to tell her this once, in a brief and fleeting "mother-daughter moment" by the kitchen sink.

"It's pretty intimidating to have you for a mom," I fumbled. "I mean, you do everything perfectly."

"Nonsense. I am not perfect," she snapped. "I am perfectly normal." See, she even does *normal* perfectly!

Not-So-Great Expectations

For the first three years Dennis and I were married, I gave it my best effort. I cooked (Mom's recipes). I sewed (Simplicity patterns). I refinished, made drapes, planted flowers. I held a full-time job, cleaned the bathrooms, washed Dennis's socks, and did my own hair. Finally one night, I sat in the middle of the (immaculate) bathroom floor and screamed at my innocent husband.

"I cannot do it all!" I sobbed. "It's unreasonable for you to expect it of me."

"*I* don't expect it of you," Dennis replied calmly. "*You* expect it of you. You are not your mother, and until you come to grips with this fact, you are going to keep driving yourself crazy."

Well I must admit, for a guy who most of the time can't even make his own ham sandwich, Dennis sure has his moments, and when he does, they can be piercing. He was right: I'm not my mother. And over the years, I've gradually gotten it through my head that this is okay. I hate to sew, but I love to garden. I'm a great cook, but I'm pretty lousy at cleaning up. I can't do my own hair, but I have a hairstylist friend whom I've trusted for fifteen years. And I like the way clothes smell, fresh out of the dryer. Accepting all these differences has helped me to love myself, and it has also helped me to love my mother for the great woman she is.

Chances are that you, too, are reacting to your mother's way of doing things. My mother is reacting to her mother. Most of us are trying desperately to be exactly like our mothers, or nothing at all like them. My friend's mom was an alcoholic, an emotional incompetent. Cindy has spent her adult life proving that she is just the opposite.

Our mothers, in one way or another, made us who we are. So did our fathers. The way our parents raised us, taught us, loved us (or didn't) has a profound impact on our self-esteem and our achievements. So do a lot of other things—our inborn temperament, the region where we grew up. Even our birth order is a factor.

I was a first child—a "good" child. The one who sought to please. The one who took the first steps, made the first grades, went on the first dates, left home first. Maybe it was hard to be my little brother; but believe me, it wasn't easy to be first either.

Report cards were a big deal at my house. My parents expected *A*s. When I made a B, they sat me down and asked me just what had *happened* here. Why hadn't I done my best?

I remember once telling my dad that Nancy Lewis got a dollar for every A she got on her report card, and what did he think of that idea?

"I'll tell you what," he replied. "Why don't you try making something other than an A, and see what you get?"

You can see how it was.

In our house, the worst thing you could be was average. That kind of standard has both a good and a bad side. Working "above average" is a great goal, but it can be daunting; it can make you afraid to try at all. I dropped a couple of classes in college because it was obvious I wasn't going to make a good grade. It seemed better to get out than just to get by. I wasn't going to attempt what I couldn't excel in.

I've seen this attitude in my oldest son. Seth had the hardest time practicing his piano lessons because he hated to make a mistake. Sometimes he hesitated to try a new song because he couldn't get it right the first time. My youngest, Ben, spent a frustrating year in first grade trying to "be good." One day he sobbed, "It's too hard, Mommy. I can't be good enough." What could I say? Neither can I.

Dennis and I are trying to downplay accomplishment in our house and emphasize effort—to teach our children that some-times things are worth doing for their own sake, not just to be "the best." This is hard for two perfectionists; we don't always lead by example. But there is a distinct difference between *being* the best and *doing our* best. This applies to grades, sports, parenting, weight loss, or anything else. We can't compare our success to the next guy's. Everybody's best effort is different. And the thing is, in real life you can't always drop the course in mid-semester if things aren't going well. You have to keep doing some things, even if you find you're not going to make an A—things like laundry, housekeeping, and dieting. Things like parenting or marriage.

We are all good at some things and not so good at others. Nobody can do it all—especially not perfectly, and certainly not all at once!

A Time for Everything

I used to loathe that "excellent wife" described in Proverbs 31. She works with her hands, brings her food from afar, rises while it is still night, considers a field and buys it, extends her hand to the poor. Her clothing is fine linen. She smiles at the future and opens her mouth in wisdom. Her children rise up and bless her.

Ugh! This is not someone you'd want as a next-door neighbor. My kids do not rise up and call me blessed. Most days they just rise up and call me for breakfast.

I've come to realize that this passage doesn't describe this woman's "to-do" list for a day; it describes what she's accomplished through the course of her whole life.

"There is a time for everything," wrote the author of Ecclesiastes, "and a season for every activity under heaven" (Eccl. 3:1). In a woman's life are many seasons. There is time for a career, a time for having babies, a time to drive carpools, a time to worry over teenagers. There is a season for the "empty nest," for a second honeymoon, for grandchildren, and for taking care of our own aging parents. There is time for a spotless house, for gardening, for getting degrees and volunteering, for teaching a Sunday School class. There is time for cooking, laundry, reading, taking walks, taking naps, and going out to dinner. But not all at once.

Each season has its rewards and blessings, its struggles and pain. And each is only for a *season*. The trick is to learn to say, "What time is it?" — then to let go of the things for which there is no time right now.

Human Doings

Claire wrote to me once that we ought to be called "human doings" instead of "human beings" because we measure our days by what we get done. The great thing about heaven, Claire remarked, is that we will finally have the time just to *be*. There'll be time to sit together, to talk, to sing one more chorus of our favorite hymn, with all the harmonies. Best of all, we'll have time just to be with Jesus — and this is the reason for which we were created — to *be* with Him.

I don't think Jesus kept a "to-do" list (Monday 11:30: Heal blind man. 2:15: Cast out demon. Tuesday: Stop by temple and rebuke Pharisees.). I think He was who He was — and who He was, was God. God whose handshake could heal leprosy. God whose dinner conversation revealed eternal secrets. God who let children sit on His lap. God who had an agenda, but always found time to stop along the way.

If you want a funny picture of the contrast between Jesus and the "human doings" who followed Him, read the Gospel of Mark. This is a fast-paced Gospel — one episode right after another, with no commercials in between. Most of the time, the disciples seem to have their tongues hanging out, and it shows in their attitudes. They come back from days of healing and teaching, get in a boat to go for a little retreat, and find a crowd waiting for them on the other side of the lake. "Send them away," we hear them groan. And later they whine, "Who's going to feed all these people?"

By contrast, Jesus never seems rushed or harried. If His retreat is interrupted, He is willing to spend all day teaching on the hillside. He is glad to stop on the road for a group of lepers, or sit by the well in deep conversation with a woman to whom nobody else will give the time of day. He senses when the crowd is getting hungry and takes measures to handle the situation. He picks up on the look in one man's eye when he asks a crucial question, hears the urgency in another's voice when the situation is desperate. And while the others are sleeping in exhaustion, He can be found alone on the mountain—praying.

Much of Jesus' ministry seemed to take place while He was going somewhere. So many stories in the Gospels begin, "As He was going..." or "While He was walking...." He got up and went through His day, and in the course of it, He was sensitive to those He encountered and was always listening to His Father. "I do nothing on my own," Jesus explained, "but speak just what the Father has taught me" (John 8:28). Jesus always knew what time it was, because He was led not by a list but by a Person. And at the end of His brief life He was able to say, "I have completed the work You gave me to do" (John 17:4, paraphrase mine).

Too Much "To Do" About Nothing

Do you have a to-do list? I bet you do. You may carry it in a daytimer, keep it on a monogrammed notepad, or scratch it on the back of an envelope. Most of us have lists of one kind or another. At the end of the day, we like to be able to cross off items and say, "I accomplished something."

A to-do list can be a great tool, helping you to focus on doing what is important in your life. Or it can tyrannize you; it can run your life. It can, at times, be a great source of guilt, if you don't get everything on your list done.

I've become quite skilled at making to-do lists. You might say I've graduated to the "advanced" level of list-making. I now have "A" lists, "B" lists, and "C" lists of things to do. I can prioritize and procrastinate with the best of them. I can justify not getting a "C" item done today by simply moving it to the "B" list for tomorrow. (I actually attended a seminar to learn how to do this.)

To be fair, there are things on my list that are very impor-tant—like everybody having clean underwear, or finishing the chapter that is due to my editor next week. I really should get these things done. But some truly important things don't usually show up on my list—such as having coffee with the friend who needs to talk, or inspecting with my son a new crop of toadstools under the bridge. These are things I should do, too, in spite of what doesn't get crossed off my list at the end of the day.

The question is not, "Did I finish everything I had to do?" but "Did I finish the work God gave me to do?"

Lord of the List

Let me offer you a way to look at your day as a human being, rather than as a "human doing." It's called "the ministry of interruption." My friend, Katherine Bryan—a woman who has accomplished many things—taught me this:

First, I write down my to-do list for the day. It looks some-thing like this:

1. Buy groceries
2. Wash whites
3. Call committee members re: Tues. mtg.
4. Finish article due on Fri.
5. Soccer 4:00
6. Bake brownies for Matt's class

I start out the morning by making my grocery list and putting in a load of laundry. Then I sit down to make my committee phone calls. "Call waiting" interrupts me, and I take the call which is from the school nurse. My neighbor's son, Martin, threw up in second period. His mother Amy is not home, and my name is on her emergency list. Can I come and get Martin?

Of course I can. I bring Martin home, make him a bed on the playroom sofa, and take his temperature. I leave a message for his mom. Then I spend the day caring for Martin, finishing the laundry and phone calls, and working on my article. Amy comes home at three o'clock, horrified to find that I've had her son all day. She gratefully takes him home. My kids come home shortly after that. I throw them in the car and head out for the grocery store and soccer practice.

On the way, I pass my friend Peggy's kids walking by the side of the road, crying. I stop. Their dog has run away; they're looking for him. Also they forgot their house key, and they're locked out. Now Peggy's a single mom; she won't be home from work until six o'clock. In late November in Nashville, it will be cold and dark outside by five. So I pile the kids in the car and drive around looking for the dog. Then I take them home with me and call Peggy to let her know I've got them.

It's too late for soccer, and there's no sign of the dog. To cheer everyone up, I bake the brownies that were meant for

Matt's class. For dinner, I throw together what Ben calls a "Manager's Special" with what I have in the fridge, since I never got groceries. Dennis comes home. Peggy arrives to pick up her kids. The day is shot.

Just looking at my to-do list, it appears that I got almost nothing done today, doesn't it? But I guarantee that my neighbors Amy and Peggy both think I did something important! I could take a second look at that list and add:

7. Help Amy with Martin today
8. Look for lost dog
9. Back up Peggy in emergency
10. Bake brownies and have fun with kids

Wow! I actually had a busy day. And I did some very important things—crucial in the lives of two other women and their families. I'm amazed that I also managed to do three loads of laundry, make my committee calls, work on my article, *and* put a meal on the table. Give me a pat on the back; I'm super!

Most important, when I go to bed tonight, I can say to my Father, "I finished the work You gave me to do."

My friend Gloria Gaither says we are all created equally in one way: We all have twenty-four hours in a day. Our challenge comes in how we spend what we've been given. And that's a tricky point, because often what is most important is not something you can check off and say, "I did that."

The bottom line is who is in charge—your Lord or your list?

I Do It!

I saw a great t-shirt that said:
LET'S GET SOMETHING STRAIGHT:
(1) THERE IS A GOD. (2) YOU'RE NOT HIM.

We sure try to be, though. We think we need to be all-knowing, all-seeing, completely capable to handle whatever comes our way. We think of ourselves as some modern version of Cinderella's fairy godmother, showing up with a magic wand, convinced that nothing is impossible. Bibbidy-bobbidy-boo— everything's fixed.

Rachel, the daughter of my friends Bob and Jane Farrell, had a thing about magic wands when she was a little girl. One Christmas, Rachel asked for a magic wand. They gave her a shiny plastic one with glitter. She bopped a few things with it and caught on that it was just pretend.

So the next Christmas Rachel was more specific; she wanted a *real* magic wand (and don't try to fake me out again). Bob and Jane thought they were being clever by giving Rachel a puppy with a note attached that said,

Dear Rachel,
I can't give you my magic wand. I need it. But here is a real puppy instead. I hope you like him.

Love, Santa

Rachel did like the puppy, but she also made it clear that he was not what she really wanted.

The third year, when the words *real magic wand* again appeared on the list, Bob and Jane tried to reason with Rachel. Wouldn't she like some other things? Toys? Dolls?

"No," Rachel replied. "If I have a magic wand, I can make my own stuff."

That's what we want. We want to make our own stuff. We don't want to have to ask, even from God, who has a lot more resources than Santa. We've become so competent at moving mountains and making things happen, we've left no room for Him to meet our needs. (Who needs to wait on the Lord, when you can buy now and pay later in installments?)

We are the two-year-old whose stubborn response is, "No! *I* do it!" It doesn't matter whether or not she really can; most of the time she can't. She doesn't care. She just doesn't want to need help. She wants to prove she is a Big Girl.

Be Still and Know

God has made it clear that we do not have to prove we are Big Girls. It is not our job to do it all; it isn't even within our power.

"I know the plans I have for you," the Lord says to us (Jer. 29:11). How will we ever know His plans if we are so busy with our own?

"Trust in the LORD with all your heart and lean not on your own understanding" (Prov. 3:5). It is His job to have all the answers; it's our job to ask the questions.

"My God will meet all your needs" (Phil. 4:19). It is His role to provide. Our role is to need.

When our son Seth was little, he had a pair of Superman pajamas, complete with a red flannel cape and a big yellow S. Every night after his bath, he would put on those "jammies," climb up on the back of the sofa, flap his cape, and jump off. He was sure he could fly. After all, he had the cape; he had the outfit. He'd seen the guy do it on TV.

We finally had to break the news to him that there is no Superman. Somebody just made him up. No matter how hard Seth flapped his cape, he wasn't ever going to fly.

I know we must look like this to our Father at times—

flapping our capes, trying so hard. "Give it up," He must want to say to us. In fact, he *has* said it: "Be still, and know that *I* am God" (Ps. 46:10).

Only One has the power to do it all. Only One has the strength we keep trying to muster, the control over time we want to possess. Only One can meet everybody's needs, has all the answers. "Be still," He says, "and know who I am. Let me show you what's important to do and what is not. Let me tell you what time it is. Let me help you with the things you're not good at. It's okay to be weak; I am strong. It's okay to be tired; lean on Me!"

I have news for you, dear reader: Superwoman is a myth. I don't care if you have seen her on TV or in a magazine. Somebody made her up. She doesn't exist, and you can't be who she is. You're just a normal woman with the same twenty-four hours as everybody else. You have your good days and your bad days. Sometimes you do it all beautifully; sometimes you don't. And don't kid yourself—it's just the same for all the rest of us. We aren't doing it all, either, no matter how hard we flap our capes.

Hey, you, with the "S" on your chest: I have an idea. Why don't we all climb down off the back of the sofa and sit together with a cup of coffee? I'm willing to ignore something on my to-do list, if you are.

Come to me,
all you who are weary and burdened,
and I will give you rest.
Take my yoke upon you and learn from me,
for I am gentle and humble in heart,
and you will find rest for your souls.
For my yoke is easy and my burden is light.

Matthew 11:28–30

Master, You are the Author of time.
Your timing is perfect.

When I find myself rushed and stressed,
I know it's because I am not listening to You.

Show me how to spend my hours, my days.
Free me from the tyranny of my to-do list.

Open my eyes and ears to the opportunities
You bring into my path,
and make me willing to be interrupted
by Your presence.

Amen

SURRENDER YOUR TO-DO LIST

Today, make a conscious effort to surrender your time and energy to God.

Pray over your schedule, your list of things to do.

Ask God to show you how *He* wants you to spend your time today.

Then keep your eyes open for the opportunities He brings your way for the "ministry of interruption"!

6

ONCE UPON A ROMANCE

Claire's chapter about marriages that weren't made in Hollywood

A good relationship has a pattern like a dance, and is built on some of the same rules. The partners do not need to hold on tightly because they move confidently in the same pattern. . . . To touch heavily would be to arrest the pattern and freeze the movement, to check the endlessly changing beauty of its unfolding. There is no place here for the possessive clutch, the clinging arm, the heavy hand; only the barest touch in passing. Now arm in arm, now face to face, now back to back. . . . They are partners moving to the same rhythm, creating a pattern together and being invisibly nourished by it.

— Anne Morrow Lindbergh

I'll never forget a telephone call that woke me from a sound sleep a number of years ago.

"Hurro," I muttered thickly into the receiver.

"Mom, is that you?" Andy wanted to know.

"Yes, I think so," I answered sleepily.

"What're you doin'?" he inquired (a bit inappropriately, I thought).

"Andy," I growled, squinting one bloodshot eye at the neon dial of the bedside clock, "It's three-twenty-two in the morning. What do you *think* I'm doing? I'm sleeping. Or at least I *was* sleeping...What are *you* doing?"

"Mom," he answered excitedly, "I just got up off my knee from asking the foxy and adorable Jenni Uplinger to be my bride. And the foxy and adorable Jenni Uplinger has just responded in the affirmative!"

"Oh, Andy!" I gushed, all hostility at being awakened suddenly gone. We dearly love Andy's Jenni, and to tell the truth, I was not overly surprised. Andy had been asking an awful lot of questions lately about "how to know that you know that you know she's the one."

"Jenni wants to talk to you, okay?"

"Put her on," I answered.

"Mrs. Cloninger," said the sweet, young voice on the other end. (Since that night I've been encouraging her to call me "Claire," and she has been trying her hardest.)

"Hi, Jenni," I responded.

"Mrs. Cloninger," she began again, "Andy told me you've been praying for his wife-to-be ever since he was a little boy."

"That's right. I have."

"Well, I guess you didn't know who you were praying for all those years. And I sure didn't know there was someone praying for me. But now that I do know, I'd like to thank that someone."

Tears filled my eyes. The answer to my prayer was calling to thank me for praying! Oh, God, You are so awesome!

I remember not being able to go back to sleep that night. Thoughts and images tumbled through my mind. I could see Andy as a married man. I could see Jenni's fresh, pretty face, and I praised God for the joy of having a "daughter" to love. I could see their children running and laughing and climbing up on the knee of ...who was that wrinkled, gray-haired woman? No, don't go there...not yet.

Quickly changing mental channels, I let my mind begin to wander back through the beginnings of my own marriage. And as I did, I began to look for something—some harvest of wisdom from our decades of experience as husband and wife—something weighty and profound that I could pass along to my son and new daughter (should it ever occur to them to ask for such a thing). Considering how much time had elapsed since I had first dreamed of being a bride, I couldn't help thinking that surely I must have learned a little something.

Seeking the Fairy-Tale Scenario

If there is one area of life in which most of us yearn for a fairy-tale scenario—and if there is one area of life in which our expectations get totally out of line with reality—it's the area of love and marriage. Little girls, especially, learn to look for the arrival of the "one and only" the way a drowning man looks for a boat. By the time we're of dating age, most of us have watched a million movies that conclude with the scene where the boy gets the girl. (Rarely do we get to see this same couple fifteen years later, when he's lost his job and his hair, she's having an identity crisis, and the oldest child has just entered adolescence!)

Like most little girls, I fantasized about having a fairy-tale wedding. My sister, Ann, and I had a costume trunk at the foot of our bed from which we could pull together authentic-looking bridal regalia in a matter of seconds. I had made hundreds of pretend trips down the aisle by the time I decided to go for the real thing.

Like most little girls, too, I had focused the greatest part of my attention on the wedding, and little or none on the marriage. Living with someone through good and bad 'til death-do-us-part were words in a game of make-believe, not the kind of commitment I was in any way prepared to make back then.

I wonder if anyone comes into this life naturally equipped with the unselfish kind of love that is required for a happy marriage. I certainly didn't. I arrived with a "what's in it for me?" attitude. (I believe this is what is known as the fallen condition of humanity!)

My parents raised me to share my toys and be kind to the new girl at school and put part of my allowance in the collection plate on Sunday. A generous spirit did not come naturally, but by the time I was old enough to date I had acquired an exterior that was sufficiently civilized to gain entrance into many social situations and most public places. Underneath this polite exterior, however, I was still very much out for "number one."

I sincerely believed that what I wanted was to fall madly in love with the perfect person and live for him and him only. I couldn't wait to share my all with him and make him happy for the rest of his life. (I didn't know it at the time, but what I really wanted under this facade of self-sacrifice was to have this perfect person live for me and me only, share his all with me, and make *me* happy for the rest of *my* life!)

What I was waiting for, by and large, was that larger-than-life, idyllic Hollywood romance to materialize out of nowhere, thereby eradicating boredom, bad news, depression, heartburn, hangnails, and other assorted negative stuff. I fully believed that a prince had been dispatched in my general direction. It was only a matter of time. My foot was poised and ready for that glass slipper.

A Prince Named "Spike"

Instead, I fell in love with Spike.

Spike is not his real name. His real name is Robert Arrington Cloninger. He is named for his father, Robert, and for his maternal grandmother, whose maiden name was Arrington. To me, this name is strong yet sensitive, down-to-earth yet ethereal, practical yet beautiful. Unfortunately, however, he has never been called Robert Arrington, or even Robert, even in passing. When he was an infant in arms, one of his uncles dubbed him "Spike," and the name stuck.

I've always known Spike. Long before I entered kindergarten, Spike was at most of the birthday parties I attended. His parents and my parents were friends. His best friend, Danny, was my next-door neighbor, so Spike was always in our backyard, or so it seemed. He was part of the neighborhood scene, a familiar character in the drama of my childhood.

Spike taught my little brothers to shoot basketball. When I was fourteen, he and Danny taught me to water ski. (They simply wouldn't let me back in the boat until I managed to get up on the skis!) Spike and I performed together in our elementary-school chorus production of *H. M. S. Pinafore,* and in high school we sang a duet entitled "Pretty Baby" in the Key Club Minstrel.

Though we had a few dates back in those days, they were not of the romantic variety. In fact, we were such chums to each other that neither of us even considered these outings a "date."

Usually Spike would call at the last minute and say something like, "I can't get a date for tomorrow. You wanna go out?" As unflattering as that might sound to you, it didn't wound or surprise me one bit. After all, this was my old buddy Spike.

So if anyone back then had told me I'd be marrying Spike
Cloninger some day, I would have been pretty disappointed. I
was on the lookout for somebody tall, dark, and mysterious,
who would sweep into my life one day and carry me off into
that distant and romantic locale known as "happily ever after."
Instead, Spike (who was tall, dark, and anything but mysterious) came home from the Army one summer, so handsome
and grown up and comfortably dear that I fell for him in spite
of myself.

I married Spike in the middle of my junior year at Louisiana
State University. We knew we'd have only three months to live
together as married people before he'd have to go overseas for
thirteen months—without me. It was a less-than-optimal situation for newlyweds. But we were so blissful (and let's face it, so
ignorant) that it seemed like an almost romantic dilemma. I
quit school and we rushed headlong into the big middle of it.

We married in February and moved immediately to Ft. Knox,
Kentucky. There we had three fun-filled months during which
Spike learned to be an armor commander and I learned the dif-
ference between paprika and chili powder.

Then the next thing we knew, he was leaving for what the
Army called a "hardship tour" in Korea. And I was moving
home to Louisiana to live with Mom and Dad for thirteen
months—which turned out to be something of a hardship tour
in itself.

Not that Mom and Dad weren't great. But Mom describes my
life that year pretty accurately when she says that I had become
a "swoose"—that is to say, not a swan and not a goose. I didn't
fit in with my single friends since I wasn't single. And I didn't
fit in with the few married couples my age whom I knew, since the
other half of my "couple" was on the other side of the globe.

Spike's homecoming thirteen months later was very exciting, but also very difficult for both of us. Here we were, sixteen months into this marriage, but we had actually lived together only three short months. Here we were, supposed to know each other so well, when actually we had both changed dramatically during the thirteen months we had been apart. Here we were, one flesh, but feeling more like total strangers.

I really struggled that first year after Spike's return. He was extremely busy with his Army responsibilities, and I was in a new place without any family or friends for the first time in my life. I didn't know how to talk to him about what I was going through or what I needed, and I'm sure I wasn't much good at listening to his needs, either.

What's more, I felt guilty about not being happy. I know this probably sounds dumb, but I was certain that I was doing something wrong. I thought that newlyweds were supposed to feel all "glowy" and perfect, but I was feeling mostly lonely and confused. What was wrong with me?

All the childhood games I had played, dressing up in a white veil and carrying a bouquet, had not prepared me for the realities of making a life with another human being. All the bride magazines I had read about having the picture-perfect ceremony and reception had neglected to mention what happens after the guests go home.

Not a Happening, but a Discipline

I may have been more naïve than many people, but I don't really think my story is that unusual. Most people are not really prepared for marriage or what it will be like. Lots of us have one kind of person in mind, and end up marrying another. Others walk down the aisle with what they assume to

be "the person of their dreams," only to discover, months or
years into the marriage, that their perfect dream of a partner
has acquired some of the elements of a nightmare!

More often than not, the dream marriage (like the dream
partner) will run into its nightmare moments as well. There
will be unexpected adjustments to be make — unplanned-for
bumps and disagreements and areas of conflict. I don't know
anyone who has been married any length of time at all who
would describe marriage as a totally smooth sail into the sunset
of their expectations. It's not a picnic. Or as Calvin Miller once
said, it's "not a happening, but a discipline."

And yet, despite the fact that our romance and marriage has
not exactly followed the "glass slipper scenario" — despite the
fact that it has had more real life to it than fairy tale — I
wouldn't have missed being married to Spike Cloninger for the
world. This marriage is where I've grown up. It's where I've
found my faith. It's been the sandpaper the Lord has used to
rub the rough edges off of us both and make us into more of
what He had in mind for us as individuals. And with some of
the rough edges off, after more than three decades, we finally
do fit together as one.

A Major Hurdle to Oneness

Arriving at "oneness" doesn't happen without your having
to get over some hurdles. One of the major hurdles to oneness
that I observe in marriages is that each partner brings with him
or her the history, experiences, values, prejudices, and temperaments of other lives. When two persons marry, their parents and grandparents inevitably get into the act.

Look back with me at our families of origin, and you'll see
what I mean. (Don't worry — I didn't bring the family slides!)

I grew up in a frame house on a shady street with two
parents and four siblings. My mama, Virginia, was an only
child, raised by an alcoholic father and a highly emotional
mother. Mom is artistic, introverted, perceptive, intelligent,
sensitive, shy, and loving. She can be pensive and sometimes
melancholy. She has a great sense of humor.

Charlie, my dad, was the older of two boys from his father's
first marriage. His mother died of pneumonia when Dad was
five, so he was raised by an aunt and uncle in a small town.
Somewhere in those bumpy and unstable years, Dad decided it
would be a good idea always to try looking on the bright side.
He is an extrovert—practical, energetic, action-oriented, and
stubbornly optimistic. He's a good listener and a good friend.

Mama's family, the Wheadons and Kilpatricks, were from
north Louisiana. They were English and Scotch-Irish. Dad's
family, the deGravelles, were from the French area of south
Louisiana (which might as well be a different country!).

Spike's parents, Marjorie and "Dobbin" (yes, his name was
Robert, too), were from a little town in North Texas named
Electra. Marjorie was a delightful combination of the personalities of her parents. (Her mom was a dreamer and her father
was a practical and pragmatic man's man.) Marjorie was raised
to believe that everything is possible, and she invariably
proved this to be true. A five-foot-tall dynamo, sunny and outgoing, Marjorie never met a stranger. She was strong, compassionate, and sometimes blind to the faults of those she loved.

Dobbin was from a family of ten children. His father was one
of those big, tough, thoroughly masculine Texans who would
rough and tumble and tease the grandchildren mercilessly. I
never heard Dobbin's mother, Effie, say a single word. (After
raising ten children, no wonder. She was probably just plain

worn out!) She wore simple cotton house-dresses and her hair in a knot, and was usually doing some kind of handwork while everyone else was talking.

I often wondered how Dobbin, raised by shy, retiring Effie, adjusted to his bubbling, outgoing bride, but he did. Dobbin was kind, romantic, stubborn, gentle, and one of the humblest men I've ever known.

The above paragraphs list just a few facts about Spike's parents and mine, which I've reported succinctly and rather unemotionally. But these are not unemotional facts. We are the components of four unique, specific individuals — our parents. We are the raw ingredients of their two marriages as well as the components that were programmed into our own.

And so, even though it seemed in the beginning that our marriage (Spike's and mine) was a combination of only two lives, we gradually discovered that it was actually a combination of many lives. Because of this, when we began to relate to each other as husband and wife, we sometimes found that the conflicts in our marriage were not actually between the two of us as individuals. They were, instead, a clash between some hand-me-down preference of his family's and some inherited idea from mine!

I started married life with the naïve assumption that our life together would be like an empty suitcase that we would pack with all the beautiful treasures that love would lead us to discover. In actuality, we arrived on our honeymoon with a lot of extra baggage already packed — beliefs and traits and tendencies we'd acquired from our families. The challenge in our marriage has been in the careful unpacking of each other's bags — delighting in some of the wonderful things we find in each other, making peace with others, and making a joint decision to throw a few things overboard!

Jenni and Andy, too, would arrive on their honeymoon with "extra baggage" and emotional "heirlooms"—some from Jenni's family and some from ours. And they will spend their lifetime together as husband and wife unpacking the treasures and the white elephants of each other's personalities—polishing and appreciating, reupholstering and rearranging, to make a comfortable blend of all the traits and qualities they'll learn to treasure in each other.

I wish I knew some magic formula for making the process of "unpacking their lives" totally painless. If such a formula were in my possession, I would already have patented it—and be rolling in the dough! Unfortunately, as far as I know, such a formula doesn't exist.

But over our many years of marriage (thirty-seven this February), I have gained a kernel or two of insight. I offer these gladly and freely to any and all who have decided to embark on this journey of the heart, as well as to all of those who are already on the trip.

(Come to think of it, maybe each mother-in-law should write a marriage chapter, neatly typed and double-spaced, containing every bit of advice she'd ever want to give to the kids. Then instead of butting in with lots of verbiage and helpful hints, she could just calmly suggest "page seven, paragraph three," and then shut up!)

Kernels of Insight

What did I think I was getting myself into that long-ago Saturday morning, February 23, 1963, when I took my dad's arm and walked down the long, polished center aisle of the Episcopal church to link my life with Spike Cloninger? What did I believe and hope and expect my marriage to be that it has not been? And what has it been that I never expected?

Misconception #1: The Degree-of-Difficulty Theory

To begin with, I thought marriage would be easier. I thought we'd fit together more or less automatically, like Barbie and Ken. I thought love would glide us through the "bonding process" without a hitch. Or at the very least, I thought that any struggles would simply take on the romantic sheen of a classy melodrama in which we had been cast as the romantic leads.

But I have found that very little seems to happen automatically in a marriage relationship. Marriage is *work*—sometimes gritty, sweaty, uncomfortable work. In fact, I figure that the degree of difficulty in combining two lives ranks somewhere between rerouting a hurricane and finding a parking place in downtown Manhattan.

I am of the opinion that only God Himself can make a marriage happen really well. And when He does it His way, it's one of His very best miracles. I mean, the Red Sea was good, but for my money, this is better. What God can create out of the combined ingredients of two surrendered lives is indeed "infinitely more than we ever dare to ask or imagine" (Eph. 3:20 PHILLIPS).

Misconception #2: The Clairvoyant Spouse Theory

When I was a newlywed, I thought that if Spike really loved me, he should be clairvoyant (or at least Claire-voyant!). He should automatically *know* what I was thinking and feeling and what I needed without my verbalizing a thing. If my needs weren't being met exactly as I felt they should be, I would jump to the conclusion that he didn't love me.

It was an enormous breakthrough for me to realize that Spike really wanted to be there for me. He wanted to be able to meet my needs the best he could. But he wasn't a mind-reader. He couldn't know what I needed unless I told him!

And so, over the years, we've gotten better and better at sharing our thoughts and feelings, clarifying our hopes, needs, and expectations for each other and our relationship. As a consequence, we've gotten better at meeting each other's needs and helping each other realize some of those hopes and expectations.

Misconception #3: The Key-to-Happiness Theory

Before I was married, I thought being happy meant getting what you want. I have learned, after thirty-seven years of marriage, that being happy means loving what you get.

Misconception #4: The Beef-Stew Theory

In the early years of our marriage, when we were both in school and working a couple of jobs and not seeing nearly enough of each other, I had the misconception that a marriage can survive that kind of benign neglect.

I've learned since then the truth of what my friend Chris Kelly always says: Making a marriage is a lot like making a stew; it will only be as good as the ingredients you put into it. If you are not taking time for long talks and long walks together, for special dinners and afternoons off, for laughter and romance and celebrating each other, your marriage is going to be a bland and watery dish indeed.

Misconception #5: The Major Moments Theory

I somehow assumed early on that the most important days in a marriage would be the anniversaries, the weddings, the

Christmases, and the family reunions. I have found instead that the most important day in any marriage is today!

My dear friend Mr. George told me something when he was a very old man—something I've never forgotten.

"Claire," he said, "Don't wait to be happy. Don't put it off. Martha Lee and I were always going to take a fancy trip out of California when Bubby was through with college. We never made it to California."

He chuckled a little, sadly shaking his head. I imagine he was remembering his Martha Lee. And then he said, "Call up Spike right now. You two ought to go out and do something wonderful together . . . tonight!"

Misconception #6: The Grin-and-Bear-It Theory

I've got to confess that I used to have a major misconception about God and marriage. I thought that if we do get stuck in a lousy marriage, God wants us to hang on by the skin of our teeth and simply gut it out until the bitter end. I was wrong about this—terribly wrong. This is not what God wants at all. He wants us to stay together, all right. But it's not enough just to gut it out. He wants us to stay and pray and work and keep loving. He wants us to hope and believe in what He can do in us. He wants us to give Him all the time and space He needs to make that lousy marriage into something not just tolerable, but beautiful and brave and strong—something that will witness to His mercy and His presence in this world.

I think He's saying something to married couples, if we will just hear Him: "Don't settle for a bad marriage, or even a mediocre one. Don't lower your expectations. Raise them! Trust Me! I'm still a God of miracles!"

Well, there you have it—all the wisdom it took me thirty-seven years to put together. I can just hear you saying, "That's it??? Thirty-seven years, and she gives us The Beef-Stew Theory?"

Okay, Okay. So cut me some slack. I'm still down here in the trenches, trying to figure it out for myself!

This reminds me of a sign that Auntie Ann's friend, Susan, has on her desk. It says, "This is a test. It is only a test. If it were your actual life, you would have been given better instructions."

That's kind of how I feel about marriage. No one gives you five foolproof steps for assembling a lasting relationship. Yet you stand at the altar together, boldly promising to love, cherish, honor, and so forth, till death do you part. Pretty scary stuff!

But I remember sitting at the weddings of both my sons, filled with a tremendous sense of hope and joy. I believe in my children and in their wives and in this awesome institution of marriage that God has given us. But what's more important, I believe in God Himself. It's His power we can lean into when the going gets tough. And His grace is the best road map any of us can have to a happy marriage.

Arise, my darling,
my beautiful one, and come with me.
See! The winter is past;
the rains are over and gone.
Flowers appear on the earth;
the season of singing has come,
the cooing of doves
is heard in our land.
The fig tree forms its early fruit;
the blossoming vines spread their
fragrance.
Arise, come, my darling;
my beautiful one, come with me.

Song of Songs 2:10–13

Father, thank You for this man, just as he is.
Thank You for putting us together and
bringing us this far.
Help us not to take each other for granted.
Give us the courage to share our heartaches
and our joys,
the compassion to hold each other up and affirm each other.
Give us the strength to defend each
other and, especially, the grace to forgive each other.

Help us to raise our expectations
and look for Your miracles in our marriage.
Keep us turning back to You through it all.

Amen

CELEBRATE YOUR MARRIAGE

Make a date with your husband for a special night of reminiscing. Cook his favorite meal. (Go on, go for it — candles, linen napkins, the works!)

Get out your wedding album and spend time together looking at those fresh young faces and sharing your memories. Or get out some old love letters and read them to each other.

Think about the persons you were when you fell in love. What were each of you hoping for? What opinions, traits, and attitudes were packed in your "suitcases" when you arrived on your honeymoon? How have they changed, or how would you like to see them change?

Share your worst memory and your best.

Pray for each other. Congratulate each other on coming this far together — even if you have only a few months of married life under your belt!

Now look ahead. Plan something fun you can do together — soon!

7

WHISTLE WHILE YOU WORK

Karla's chapter about dirty socks—and other
ministries of motherhood

*Big deal.
I'm used
to dirt.*

—Erma Bombeck,
*on what she wanted
on her gravestone*

"Why didn't anybody tell me?"
Amie wailed into the phone. In the
background I could hear one toddler
crying; the other pleading "Mommy,
Mommy, Mommy"; the dryer buzzing;
and "Blue's Clues" on the television.

In three short years, my friend had
gone from single professional to bride,
then stay-at-home mother of two. The
condo she and Todd had decorated for
their newlywed life was rapidly becom-
ing cramped with playpens, swings, walkers, and diaper pails.

"Why didn't somebody *tell* me how hard this was going to
be?" Amie whined.

Because, I thought, *we're not supposed to.* I mean, we've got
it all: the brass ring, the girlhood dream, the picket fence.
We're the lucky ones—and we're not supposed to complain
about it.

"Mother" Is Not Spelled S-L-A-V-E

Let's face it, motherhood is demanding. And don't let anybody kid you. Sure you can be a mother and still do other things; but you can never do them quite as single-mindedly as you did before. Motherhood takes over your life; it seeps into your workplace, invades your pocketbook, and completely devastates your daytimer. Whether your kids are at home or at school, at daycare or in college, you are still their mother. You are their mother when they are awake or asleep—even when you're trying to sleep. You are their mother, and they are not about to let you forget it.

Nevertheless, motherhood has been good for me. It has made me a less selfish, less me-preoccupied person. More than anything else in my life, motherhood has helped me to understand the kingdom principle of servanthood.

Now, I've never really had a problem with the idea of serving the Lord. It's serving His less-than-royal subjects that tends to stick in my craw. But that's exactly the people Jesus told us to serve! He said to His disciples, "You know that those who are regarded as rulers of the Gentiles lord it over them, and their high officials exercise authority over them. Not so with you. Instead, whoever wants to become great among you must be your servant, and whoever wants to be first must be slave of all. For even the Son of Man did not come to be served, but to serve, and to give his life as a ransom for many" (Mark 10:42–45).

My children are the chalkboard upon which God is teaching me Christ's example of serving. And it's not always easy. Those whom God would have me serve are, for the most part, whiny, messy, demanding, inconvenient, quirky, moody, and usually less than grateful. They take up a lot of my time, and track mud on my clean kitchen floor. They don't act very royal, and they hardly ever say, "Well done, good and faithful mom." It is seldom inspiring to serve them.

But Jesus said, "Whatever you did for one of the least of these brothers of mine, you did for me" (Matt. 25:40). He counts our care for each little one as service unto the King.

A Sock in My Purse

I once heard a woman speak on the subject of servanthood. She said she used to view taking care of her husband and kids as drudgery, but then she asked God to change her attitude.

"Now," she said enthusiastically, "each time I pick up my husband's or child's dirty sock from the floor, I use it as an opportunity to praise God for them."

All the women in the audience nodded and whispered "Amen!" I looked around and thought, *Am I the only one here who just doesn't get it?*

I felt so guilty for a while I even carried one of Dennis's socks around in my purse to remind me! But I have to be honest with you; while I am very thankful for my husband and children, I have never thanked God that I have to pick up their socks.

The problem with being a servant-mother is that the job is just so ordinary. So day-to-day, bread-and-butter, meat-and-potatoes. It's not very flashy. You spend all day washing, folding, and putting away clothes, and what does your family do? They wear them and get them dirty again. You slave over a hot stove (or microwave); they take one look and say, "Ew! Can't we just order a pizza?" You sweep the dirt out; they track it right back in. You make the bed; they mess it up. The process just keeps going 'round and 'round in the same dull circle.

A carpenter or gardener or even a garbage man can look back at the end of the workday and see a finished roof, a newly planted bed, a neighborhood clean and orderly. A mom looks back and sees the same stuff to do all over again. There's no monument to her hard work, no sense of an end to the job, no moving on to the next assignment. It's what Dennis's grandmother used to call "sweeping the same dirt."

But don't confuse ordinary with unimportant. Jesus didn't. He used the ordinary, common elements of everyday life to teach great truths about the kingdom: bread, water, fish, stones—stuff that everybody could understand. Jesus spent the first thirty years of His life doing the ordinary work of a stonemason, keeping the routines and responsibilities of family life. The years of His ministry were spent with ordinary people—eating with them, staying in their homes, caring for their families. "Ordinary," in Jesus' eyes, has the potential to become "eternal."

Me? A Missionary?

This comes home to me through my friend Sherri, who is a missionary in Asia, among some of the last unevangelized people in the world. Sherri and I email each other almost daily, discussing our husbands, children, joys, and frustrations. I've always been in awe of missionaries like Sherri. They must be spiritual giants—certainly nothing like you and I are. I picture Sherri backpacking up remote mountains to primitive villages, her babies strapped to her back. I imagine her preaching to natives, dragging stones from the mountainside to build a small church, scooping her water out of the cold stream. But certainly not wading around in the shallow water of the mundane.

"You are so silly," she tells me. Her mountains are four flights of stairs to their high-rise, where she lugs formula and diapers and strollers back and forth. Her prayer requests are about household budgets and lack of sleep, her children's ear infections, the mothers in her neighborhood, her husband's busy schedule.

"Wait a minute!" I reply. "That's the same stuff I deal with every day! Except, of course, that the women in my neighborhood wear jeans and drive Jeeps, and I don't have to watch every word I say in case the government is reading my email." Still Sherri has gone halfway around the world, far from family and friends, and learned a new language just to do the simple, ordinary tasks of wife, mother, neighbor, friend. Those simple, ordinary tasks, done in the name of Jesus Christ, have the power to change lives.

That same power is available to you and me. It's the same power that transformed a fisherman named Peter into a great evangelist. The same power that fed five thousand families with a little boy's lunch. The same power by which an ordinary meal of wine and bread became Christ's body and blood, flowing through our veins. Paul tells us that this power available to believers is the same power that raised Christ from the dead and seated Him on the throne! (Eph. 1:18–21)

You and I are called to pack the lunches, to set the table, to prepare the meal; and then we are called to invite Christ, who transforms these ordinary moments into places where sacred things happen. These moments come at the most unexpected times. You can't plan them. The only way to catch them is to be there for all the other dull, uneventful moments, too, because the really rare ones hide among the common, and pop out at you when you least expect them.

Christ was born in a stable. Perhaps He was born there to show us that there is no place—no thing—so secular that it cannot be made sacred by His presence. A cup of water on a hot afternoon; a Band-Aid on a scraped finger; a clean bed; a delicious, home-cooked meal—these are our offerings to the King, and they are pleasing to Him.

Just Do It

On a good day, when I've had my quiet time, when I feel close to God, when I'm in great spiritual shape, when I've had a good night's rest and a delicious breakfast, I know these things. On those days "mothering" is a calling, a ministry. But most days, in the thick of the battle, my mind is not on spiritual things. Those are the days when I'm just hoping to get everyone to bed on time, with no broken bones and nothing set on fire. I suspect you have those days, too.

I've come to the conclusion that there is a certain aspect of the servant-mother role that is not going to be inspirational or glamorous or, for that matter, gratifying. It is just stuff that has to be done, and we have to do it. It's part of the job. Sometimes servant-mothers have to get up in the morning and, as the Nike ad says, "Just do it." Not for the reward. Not for the gratitude. Not so the world will be a better place. Not because you'll be the "best Mom," or because anyone will notice (because they probably won't). Just *do* it. A servant serves because that is what she is bound to do.

You and I were bought with a price: Christ's life. We are in His debt, bound to Him. This is what Paul meant when he called himself a "bondservant of Jesus Christ" (Rom. 1:1 NKJV). We owe Christ our very lives. We can never repay Him the debt of gratitude we owe. But He has told us that what He requires of us is to serve Him by serving others. When we minister to others, we are serving Christ. (See Matthew 25:40.)

"Do you love me?" Jesus asked Peter. "Then take care of my little ones" (John 21:15–19, my paraphrase).

What's Left of My Rights?

"But what about *me*?" you may ask. "How will this help me to realize *my* potential? Will it make *me* happy? What's in it for *me*?"

Several years ago, a slew of magazine articles appeared about female corporate executives who were choosing to "downshift" their careers in order to have children—the "Mommy Track." According to these articles, this was the new trend—very chic—the ultimate expression of a woman's freedom and power.

One article interviewed the forty-year-old vice president of a major corporation, who was now going to work out of her home as a consultant so that she could, as she put it, "have the experience of motherhood." It was a part of herself that she felt she was now ready to "realize."

I had to laugh. Boy, is that woman in for a surprise! I have yet to meet a baby who is at all interested in "realizing" his mother's needs. He is much more interested in his own. I'm sure that, by now, that woman has "realized" some parts of herself she was not quite ready for!

Yes, motherhood is fulfilling. Yes, it is rewarding. It is miraculous and wonderful. It is what I've always wanted to do with my life, and what I would never exchange for all the careers in the universe. But…motherhood is *not* about fulfilling your own potential; it is about helping your children fulfill theirs. It is not about having your own needs met; it is about meeting everyone else's. It is not about what you get; it is mostly about what you give.

And this is another fundamental principle of the kingdom: you must lose your life in order to find it. The greatest must be the least. The master shall be the servant. The first shall be last. Die so that you may live. Give and you shall receive. Surrender and you are truly free.

This is a mystery; it is difficult for us to understand. It is even more difficult to live. This concept is what my young friend Amie was discovering.

Surrender or Die

I'm not talking about some warm, fuzzy surrender of your life to God. I'm not talking about being a martyr.
(Q: How many mothers does it take to change a light bulb?
A: That's all right, dear, I'll just sit here in the dark!)

I'm talking about a very deliberate, eyes-wide-open, get-down-to-brass-tacks surrender:

- Surrender your body: Pregnancy wreaks havoc on your figure, and getting up in the night can sap your energy and ruin your complexion.
- Surrender your calendar: Your children's schedules are going to crowd yours.
- Surrender your priorities: Some things you've always wanted to do are going to have to wait.
- Surrender your checkbook: Some things you can't buy or do because large chunks of your family budget are earmarked for college funds, school clothes, or braces.
- Surrender your leisure: It won't be so easy to go out to lunch or to a movie.
- Surrender the twenty-four hours in your day: Some things on your list won't get done, because someone else will need your attention.

You can make your own list of what you have to surrender now, while you are raising children. Going back to school? Writing a book? Serving on a committee? Buying a new car?

Taking a trip? Recovering the couch? Having a guest room?
Getting your nails done? Keeping a clean house? Sleeping
through the night? Having some privacy?

These are real, everyday, personal invasions of your rights.
Don't underestimate them. The mother who surrenders
them—and you may have to get down on your knees several
times a day—finds a freedom and release from the "have tos,"
"should haves," "ought to bes," "why-can't-I?s" rat race that
can make you feel like a slave rather than servant. The mother
who hasn't learned to surrender will find herself feeling defen-
sive and unappreciated, her joy replaced by a feeling of futility,
her life one long list of chores.

I know. I have been that mother. Some days I still am.

Servant of All

Jesus was our model for servanthood. He was constantly on
call. People waited for Him on mountainsides, congregated on
seashores; they accosted Him on the road, and interrupted
Him on the way to the temple. When He sat down to eat, a
crowd would gather. I am sure He understands why mothers of
young children never seem to be able to have much "quiet
time" with Him; people interrupted His prayer times, too.

Still, Jesus seemed always to respond appropriately, with the
right word or touch. He knew when to give people what they
needed and when they needed to be rebuked for asking. He
never responded out of frustration or weariness. He never said,
"In a minute," or "Not now; I'm busy."

Why?

Because Jesus knew the value of people. He loved them, and
that is why He served them—even when He knew they would
be ungrateful or unbelieving, or would even one day betray

Him. He loved people even though He knew their weaknesses full well. Jesus had come to earth out of his Father's love for these people. He knew that *they* were the whole point.

A Tale of Two Sisters

The Bible gives us a beautiful illustration of serving in the story of Jesus' friends Mary and Martha. These two sisters lived with their brother, Lazarus, in Bethany. Several times, when Jesus came through their village, He stopped at their house as a guest. It must have been a place where Jesus felt loved and accepted, where He was welcomed and made comfortable among His friends.

On the occasion described in Luke 10:38–42, Martha was knocking herself out to make sure everything was done right for her guest. I can just see her, cooking on all burners in the kitchen, making the Jewish equivalent of a Sunday pot-roast dinner with all the trimmings, while her guests laughed and relaxed in the front parlor, including her sister Mary, who was not helping Martha at all. The hotter it got in the kitchen, the more irritated Martha became. On about her fifth trip into the dining room to set something on the table, Martha had had enough.

"Lord!" she exclaimed. (I'm not sure she was just calling His name.) "Don't you care that I'm doing all the work, and Mary's just sitting here? Tell her to get up and help me!"

Jesus' reply has always baffled me.

"Martha, Martha," He answered. (Can't you just hear the tone of His voice as He takes her gently by the shoulders?) "Mary has chosen the most important thing."

I can tell you, as one who would have been in the kitchen slamming pans around, Jesus' answer wouldn't have set too well with me. Oh, fine. If we all just sit in the parlor, who do you think is going to see that we eat? I think I'll just try it this next Thanksgiving, when all fifteen of my friends and relatives are sitting in front of the Titans game on TV. I think I'll just sit down with them and put my feet up, and when they all get hungry for turkey about three that afternoon, I'll say, "Well, I've chosen the most important thing." That should go over nicely!

I need to keep in mind that Jesus was not belittling Martha's service. Martha's hospitality was one of the reasons He loved to come to her house. But Martha had a problem that you and I often have—a problem of perspective. She was so focused on the menu that she forgot whom she was preparing it for. She was so preoccupied with the table-setting that she forgot about who would sit there. While she was in the kitchen making gravy, God Himself was a guest in her living room!

Jesus was reminding Martha that she had forgotten whom she was serving.

I've had trouble remembering that, too—especially during a 3:00 A.M. feeding, or when my child throws up on me in the middle of the night. When they're fighting in the back seat of the car, or when I pick up the fourteenth pair of dirty socks.

I forget, until I stop slamming pans and sit down with them. Until I watch them through the kitchen window, playing in the backyard, and marvel at their imaginations. Until I see Matt gracefully catch a ball, or Ben brings me a picture he has drawn. Until I hug my 6-foot-5-inch-tall teenager and remember when Seth was only 21 inches long. When I stop being so busy, and sit down to look and listen, I do not see my children; I see Christ.

I remember whom I am serving. I remember how much I love Him, and that this is the reason I serve them. And I understand why Jesus said, "This is the most important thing."

Then the King will say to those on his right,
"Come, you who are blessed by my Father;
take your inheritance, the kingdom prepared for you
since the creation of the world.
For I was hungry and you gave me something to eat,
I was thirsty and you gave me something to drink,
I was a stranger and you invited me in,
I needed clothes and you clothed me,
I was sick and you looked after me,
I was in prison and you came to visit me."

Then the righteous will answer him,
"Lord, when did we see you hungry and feed you,
or thirsty and give you something to drink?
When did we see you a stranger and invite you in,
or needing clothes and clothe you?
When did we see you sick or in prison and go to visit you?"

The King will reply, "I tell you the truth,
whatever you did for one of the least of these brothers of
mine, you did for me."

Matthew 25:34–40

Jesus, thank You for Your example of servanthood.
Thank You for loving people so much
that You even gave Your life for us.

Teach me to love the people I serve this same way.
Help me to remember how important they are to You,
to see them as the blessings they are.

Enable me to serve them graciously,
for through them, I am serving You.

Amen

CELEBRATE SERVING

Do you have a "Red Plate" tradition at your house?

My sister-in-law gave us a red dinner plate with "You're Special Today" inscribed around the edges. We use this plate as a way to express our special appreciation for one another.

Members of our family are honored with the red plate at their place on their birthday, or when they make a hundred on a test, or sometimes when they just need to feel loved.

Pick out a special plate at your house and start a tradition of your own. Or choose one person in your family, and do something extra special for that person one day. Prepare a favorite food, tuck a "You're Special" note into their clean laundry, give them a day off from chores, or put their picture up on the refrigerator for the day.

Think of your own ways to celebrate the loved ones you take care of every day, and remember why you serve them.

8

LET YOUR HAIR DOWN, RAPUNZEL

Claire's chapter about birthdays, moving,
and other traumatic changes

---

*No one knows
what this next
year will bring.
But one thing
is sure:
He will be
with us, and He
is enough for
every difficulty
that may arise.*

—Amy Carmichael

I'll never forget the year I turned
fifty. An avalanche of change hit me
that year. I remember one morning
writing down all the changes that had
come into my life in twelve months.
When I finished writing, I was
exhausted. I read through what I
had written, and actually the changes
themselves looked pretty positive…
on paper.

Unfortunately, we do not live our
lives on paper. We live our lives where
the fact hits the feelings. And the fact
was, it had been a year of change. And
the feeling was traumatic.

To begin with, I went into a three-day decline over my
birthday. It was not like me to overreact like that. I had never
gotten weird over a birthday before. People had joked about

thirty being old, and I'd joked back. But thirty was a piece of cake. (Actually, knowing me, it was probably several pieces of cake!)

Then when I got the black balloon treatment at forty, I pretended to be offended. But I wasn't really. I mean, what did I care? Forty was great! I was busier and happier than I had ever been. Great job, great kids, great marriage.

But fifty? Fifty suddenly seemed like such a high number. I'd just never thought of connecting it in any personal way with myself. I remember when my mother was fifty. She was a perfectly beautiful, accomplished, and gracious...*old* person.

How had this gigantic milestone managed to sneak up on me without my noticing? I couldn't help thinking about something Dave Barry once said about how the aging process "is a big, sleek, jungle snake, swimming just around the bend in the River of Life. It swallows you subtly, an inch at a time, so you barely notice the signs."

I remembered, too, how Ian Bedloe, the hero of Anne Tyler's *Saint Maybe,* had always thought that old people were born that way—"that age was an individual trait, like freckles or blond hair, and that it would never happen to him."

Yes, I had definitely been caught off guard. The day of my birthday, I kept going up to the mirror and giving myself a reality check. "Hi, I'm fifty," I'd say to myself, just to see how it felt. It didn't feel good.

But it wasn't just "the birthday" that was shaking me up. There was also "the move" that had taken place four months earlier. We had moved out of the house in which we had raised our children and spent most of our married lives—the comfortable, well-loved place I knew as home. We had left behind the sidewalks where our children had learned to ride their bikes,

and the neighbors we had grown to care about…and closets—
lots of closets. And we had moved into our tiny, remote log
cabin on the river, miles from town. For eleven years it had
been our little weekend getaway, only now we would be living
there full time. One bathroom, no closets to speak of, and
forget the neighbors and sidewalks.

Granted, we were now in an unbelievably beautiful and tran-
quil setting, surrounded by acres of woods and looking out on
a spectacular view of the river forty feet below. Granted, we
had plans to expand the house. Granted, we were living Spike's
wildest and dearest dream. But the fact remained that, for
me—an incurable extrovert—this much tranquillity was going
to be hard to bear.

And it was not just the birthday, and not just the move. It
was also "the wedding." That was the year that Andy married
the foxy and adorable Jenni Uplinger. The wedding was beautiful. The girl is incredible—a dream of a daughter-in-law. Still
the territory was unfamiliar. I mean suddenly I was somebody's *mother-in-law.*

But wait—there's more! Add to the birthday, the move, and
the wedding, the "good-byes." Within months of each other,
our son Curt left for Montana to study the Bible in Youth with
a Mission, and our best friends John and Laura had moved to
South Carolina. Of course these moves were good for the
people involved.

So why did I lie across my bed after both of those good-byes
and cry like my heart would break? I remember saying out
loud to myself between sobs, "Here I am, somebody's mother-
in-law, half-a-century old, living in a log cabin in the middle of
nowhere with no children, no closets, no sidewalks, and no best
friend!"

The Unchangeable Fact of Change

Somebody very wise once said that the only unchangeable thing about life is the fact that it is constantly changing. As much as I would like to hollow out a comfortable little niche and gather my loved ones around me and stay exactly where I am, I just cannot do that. This moment is moving past me even as I am living it. The people around me are growing up and growing old. The colors of the seasons are subtly shifting and changing right before my eyes. Styles and fads are in and out almost before I've had time to catch on to them. The music industry in which I work is in a constant state of flux. Our political leaders, our media heroes, our sports idols move through our lives in an endless parade of change. Our relationships with our parents, our children, our marriage partners are constantly entering new phases that require emotional adjustments. People we have learned to love and depend on are called away, and our lives seem at times to be filled with good-byes.

And the change that affects us is not limited to events outside ourselves. Inside, too, we are constantly being drawn to new and different horizons that need to be faced, new and fearful precipices that need to be crossed, new and challenging heights that need to be scaled.

As Sue Monk Kidd put it in her book *When the Heart Waits,* "The life of the spirit is never static. We're born on one level, only to find some new struggle toward wholeness gestating within. That's the sacred intent of life, of God—to move us continuously toward growth, restoring the divine image imprinted on our soul."

What she is saying, in effect, is that God is constantly at war with our comfort zones. He never planned for us to burrow in and get cozy while living life on planet earth. He's in the business of remaking us, and there's no way we're going to go through the process of change without a measure of discomfort. It's not *supposed* to be comfortable.

I don't think I ever really understood that the discomfort of change is an inescapable part of life, especially the Christian life. Somewhere in my childhood I got the idea that it was possible and even desirable for me to become more and more schooled in the way the world works, and thus more and more settled, set, and comfortable the older I got.

In fact, I actually believed on some level that maturity means getting so familiar with life and so adept at playing its games that it would gradually begin to fit me like a comfy old pair of house shoes. I thought I'd eventually reach a place where I could breathe a deep sigh and say, "Oh, so this is how life works! Now I understand! Now I can settle back and just enjoy it."

But surprise, surprise! Reality has never matched this expectation. It has always seemed to me that the minute I catch on to one thing and get really good at it, it's over, and my expertise is no longer needed.

I had just gotten a handle on grade school, for instance, when I had to move on to junior high. I had just figured out the inner workings of junior high when I was catapulted into high school. Senior year in high school was fantastic. I was on top of it. I was a big fish. Then suddenly, my little pond was replaced by this tremendous ocean known as college, and I was furiously paddling to stay afloat, gasping for breath again.

It was the same with raising children. I recall the challenge of bringing home Curt, our first baby—juggling all the responsibilities of bathing and changing and feeding, and especially the maddening colic hour when the little fellow screamed nonstop for what seemed an eternity. I remember I had just figured out how to ease the pain of the colic hour and rock him back to sleep, when the colic vanished—never to return. My newly discovered coping mechanism was no longer required!

This is the way it seemed to be with each of my two children at each stage in their lives—infant, toddler, grade school, teenage. I would struggle desperately to learn the new territory and finally seem to master it, just in time to be thrown headlong into something new and unfamiliar.

The Bible gives us plenty of warning about this ever-changing, transient quality of life. It tells us that we, like Abraham, are "strangers" and "pilgrims," spiritual tent-dwellers. It makes it clear that God never intended us to spend every ounce of our time and energy making ourselves more and more comfortable on this planet—that we're actually all on our way to some place entirely different. (Heb. 11:13–16; 1 Pet. 2:10–12) But as with many other passages in the Bible, we ingest this information with a grain of salt and go about the business of our lives, trying to obtain earthly security and avoid change every way that we can.

The Stella in Me

The idea of resisting change reminds me of a lady I knew in the town where I was raised. Her name was Miss Stella, and she was the aunt of a friend of mine.

Miss Stella spent all of her energy constructing rigid and unchangeable patterns of living for herself and her poor husband. She evidently found some sense of comfort in the ritual quality of the life they shared. Miss Stella did the same thing at the same hour of the day on the same day of the week three hundred sixty-five days, fifty-two weeks a year. If a friend called her to go to lunch and it was her day for a manicure, she always refused; changing course was just too much for her. Her menus were the same week by week, and on Tuesday nights, when she and her husband ate out in the same restaurant, they always ordered the same thing.

Like Rapunzel locked in a tower with no way out, Miss Stella lived in a world that was close, predictable, and confining. She had walled herself in and was afraid to let her hair down. And sadly, as Miss Stella got older, arthritis set in. The joints of her body became as brittle and inflexible as the habits and patterns into which her life had become cemented.

It would be easy for me to point a finger and criticize Miss Stella's rigid little life or to laugh at her inflexible nature. But I could never do that, because there is a little bit of Miss Stella in me. I get things the way I want them, and I don't want anybody coming in and making me change.

In the mid-eighties, for example, I was part of a church that was very close to my idea of heaven. I loved the songs and the worship and the pastor and the sermons and the people and absolutely everything about it. *At last I've found the perfect church,* I thought. *I'm home. This is it. Don't anybody change a thing!*

One summer during those "golden" years, a group of us traveled to a "spiritual renewal conference" in North Carolina. In a gorgeous Smoky Mountain setting, we laughed and played together; we studied and prayed together; we celebrated our faith and our friendships. It was fantastic.

I particularly remember one cool, crisp morning when ten of us packed a picnic lunch and climbed to the top of a mountain where there was a grassy field known as a "bald." It looked exactly like the opening scene in *The Sound of Music.* The sky was amazingly blue, with huge, fluffy, cumulus clouds drifting overhead. All around us, as far as we could see, was the untouched beauty of God's world.

After running and jumping and acting as silly as children, we
spread out our blankets and had lunch together. During lunch
and for a long time afterward, we talked about the things each
of us had gone through as children. There were some tears and
some prayers.

That was when our friend Jan pulled out the grape juice and
crackers she had secretly bought at the Seven-Eleven. There
on top of that windy mountain, feeling so much a part of one
another's lives, we shared the Lord's supper.

What an incredible day! Before the sunlight began to fade,
Spike set his camera on a rock and snapped a photo of our ten
radiant faces against a backdrop of splendor.

I didn't want to come down from that mountaintop. Like
Peter on the Mount of Transfiguration, I wanted to build a few
booths and camp out for a while in the glory of the moment.

Not long ago, I found the prized photograph of that special
moment, and I realized that seven of the ten people in it had
moved away from our area! Though Spike and I are still members of the same church, the church itself has undergone many
changes. We have a new pastor. The membership has shifted
and changed. There are new ministries, new hymns and cho-
ruses, new ways of doing things. It's still a wonderful church,
but it's very different.

We could take a picture of that treasured moment in time
and put it in a frame and hold on to it. But as much as I would
have liked to, there was no way to frame and hold on to the
moment itself. God wanted to give us all a new picture, a new
vision, a new direction.

And now, in retrospect, I can see that I would have missed
His new vision. If I had dug my heels in and stayed focused on
that old photograph, it would have faded and curled around

the edges. My spiritual life would have grown stale and musty.

God was not finished with any of us. That's why we had to come down from the mountain and go on.

Follow Me

When Jesus called to the men and women of the world He walked through, He was calling them to get unstuck. He was calling them to break loose from the safe and the predictable and the familiar. He offered no road maps, no guarantees. He simply said, "Follow me!"

Some, like Peter and Andrew and Matthew, did just that. They followed. They left their jobs and their families and their hometowns. They walked off from all that was familiar and dear.

Others, like the rich young ruler, turned their backs on Jesus and walked sadly away from Him and His kingdom. Their lives were so deeply lodged in the good things of this world that they couldn't risk the change.

In my journey so far, I've been cast in both roles. There have been times when I've followed. And there have been times when I've hung back, too afraid to let go, too terrified of the change. And from doing it both ways, I've discovered something important.

The times I've hung back and refused to change, I've found myself bogged down in a stagnant, lifeless pond, cut off from "the living water"—the cool, exhilarating waters of God's abundant mercy. Sometimes the currents have been swift and challenging; sometimes I've gotten cold or tired or uncomfortable. But I've experienced the excitement of being "unstuck." And I've known the joy of moving on with Him.

True confession time. For years I resisted moving to the

country. For years after I heard God calling and felt Him nudging us to do it, I held back. I put on my spiritual brakes and spent all kinds of energy inventing creative rationales for why we should stay in town. I'm ashamed even to put this in writing, but it's true.

I was clinging to my possessions, to my neighborhood, to my own specifications and requirements for the kind of lifestyle that I felt I needed in order to be safe and comfortable. And God didn't force me to move. He just let me experience what it feels like to be out of the center of His will.

During those years, I began to get the feeling that my life was on hold. I was sitting there, waiting for God to pick up the phone, but I was not hearing much from Him. And though I was still praying and progressing by inches in some other areas of my life, nothing much was taking place overall.

"What's wrong, God?" I would ask. "Where are You? Tell me what to do." But He had already told me what to do, and I just wasn't doing it!

Finally deciding to move was like uncorking the stopper in a bottle. It shook things loose. It got our lives back into action. Almost from the moment we put the "For Sale" sign in front of our house in town, we could feel the flow of the Holy Spirit again.

In our years since moving to the country, God has done amazing things in our lives. Spike, who was always the best artist in our high school but had never had time to spend developing that gift, now has a studio where he works with wood, creating museum-quality wooden vessels—beautiful bowls and urns and vases. His work is sold in galleries and art shops, and he enjoys showing at juried art shows. Every morning he wakes up and says, "I love my life! I wonder what I'll make today!"

I have written a book about our move to the country,
A Place Called Simplicity. It deals honestly with my struggles
to simplify, but also lays out the surprising joys I have found in
the midst of these struggles. I frequently receive letters and
emails from readers who assure me that this book has helped
them slow down and put God at the center of things.

We can never tell what God has for us, or exactly why. But
we can be certain that whatever it is, it will be for our good and
for His glory. Looking back on my reluctance to follow His
call, I see now how foolish I was. Clinging to my own stubborn
plans when God was trying to move me into His plan was like
continuing to eat stale, rotting leftovers when a bountiful ban-
quet had been set out for me. Or to use an old Bob Benson
analogy, it was like clinging to my own stale, brown-bagged
bologna sandwich at the church picnic, when the best cook in
town had invited me to sit on her homemade quilt and share
her fried chicken, potato salad, freshly baked bread, and blue-
berry tarts!

Never Say Never

Still I can't say I was surprised at the difficulties that our
change posed for me. Our move was nothing I would ever have
thought of doing on my own. In fact, I could never have even
imagined myself living in a town of three hundred and fifty
people!

Spike and I used to drive through little country towns like
this one on our way to somewhere else, and I would frequently
comment, "Who lives in these places? I could never live in a
place like this. I'd go nuts."

Have you ever noticed that God is not really interested in
pampering our preferences and prejudices? I am learning the

hard way never to say never! I am learning that God knows better than I do what needs to be added to or subtracted from my life, and sometimes His idea of change involves the very thing that seems least desirable to me. God is going after our whole hearts. And when we draw a line in the dirt and say, "I could never do that," that is often the very place He'll call for a surrender.

God's hand of change almost always requires me to let go of something I have held dear or viewed as important or known for a fact. It calls me to let go of my own agenda, my own preferences and prejudices and ultimatums. It requires a yielding of my expectations and a welcoming of His reality. And it forces me to admit that I am not the expert on every subject, not even my own life.

Mary and Martha had a very specific agenda as they waited for Jesus to arrive at their home in Bethany. They were waiting for Him to heal their brother, Lazarus, who was seriously ill. So when Jesus was late and Lazarus died, Martha was not only grief-stricken; she was also more than a little bit annoyed with Jesus for not following her plan.

"If You had been here [as You were *supposed* to have been], this would not have happened," she told Him.

But all along Jesus had a different agenda. Martha and Mary were forced to let go of their own understanding of death and to trust Jesus to bring an incredible change into their lives.

"I believe that You are the Christ, the Son of God, who was to come into the world," Martha finally acknowledged. And it was at this point that He raised her brother from the dead. (John 11:1–43)

Peter, too, had to let go of a "know-it-all" attitude. If there was one thing that Peter understood, it was fishing. After all, he was a professional fisherman. So when Jesus suggested that he change his method of catching fish, Peter was somewhat indignant.

"Master," he said, in effect, "we've been working here all night long to catch fish. If there were any fish here, we would have caught them."

But when Peter was finally willing to stop being the authority on his own life, willing to try things Jesus' way, the result was a huge catch of fish—so large that it split Peter's nets (Luke 5:1–11). And I can't help but speculate that this was the Lord's way of preparing Peter to follow orders on faith as a future "fisher of men."

The Inconvenient, the Unexpected, and the Miraculous

God's changes in our lives frequently clash with our own idea of what would be best. They are often inconvenient and unexpected and difficult to deal with.

I remember some years back when my friend Nancy's life seemed nicely on course. At age forty-three, she was near the end of her Ph.D. program. Her children were progressing into adulthood. Her marriage was a happy one. Life was good.

When Nancy began to notice some changes in her body, her first thought was, "Oh, so this is 'the change of life' I've heard so much about." Little did she know just what a change of life this would be! Nine months later little Patrick was born. Nancy's well-ordered life was suddenly filled with cribs and bibs and midnight feedings. But in the midst of the chaos, Nancy and her husband, Don, discovered the joy of one of God's unexpected miracles.

Seeing Nancy and Don with little Patrick back then,

I couldn't help but think of how Abraham and Sarah must have felt when little Isaac finally came along after all those years of waiting. Certainly he was wanted. But how convenient is the arrival of any baby, much less one born to a couple of senior citizens?

Still I'll bet Isaac kept Abraham and Sarah young in the same way that Patrick has kept Nancy and Don young. Change keeps our spiritual joints from stiffening. Just as our bodies look and feel younger when we work at staying flexible, we remain young at heart when we stay mentally and spiritually flexible to welcome God's unexpected changes.

Change on Top of Change

But sometimes change can throw a major curve to even the most flexible among us. When changes come in twos and threes, one after another, they can leave us floundering. Every change involves stress. And medical science has proven that multiple changes produce a kind of cumulative stress that, in turn, can cause anything from minor emotional upset to severe physical illness.

I believe this is what happened to me the year I turned fifty. None of the changes was really bad, but one after another they hit me and left me reeling.

I remember a time when my physical workouts provided me with a painful analogy to the cumulative effect of change. I had spent a Saturday night in Mobile with a friend, and was jogging in her lovely, historic neighborhood the next morning before church. It was a beautiful day, and I was thoroughly enjoying running past all the renovated Victorian homes and gardens. What I didn't take into account was that the roots of the huge oak trees in this old section of town had grown up under the sidewalks and had broken through the concrete in places, causing buckling and bumps. Being unfamiliar with my route, I should have been watching my step instead of gaping at the scenery. Hitting one of those bumps head-on with the toe of my running shoe, I went sprawling facedown on the sidewalk. Both elbows, both knees, and both hands were ripped open with painful brush burns.

Then, before the wounds had even had a chance to heal, I did it again! While I was running on a sandy road near our cabin, just four days later, I tripped on a root and fell again. Not only were my injuries reopened, but they were now also full of sand. Ouch!

In some sense, this is exactly what had happened to me in the spiritual realm during my year of changes. Before I had even had time to heal from one change, here came another... and another. It was the cumulative effect that really knocked me flat.

Spike refers to this analogy as "the parable of the scab." He says he especially likes to hear me tell it at the dinner table! But although it is not an appetizing tale, the "scab parable" does teach a pretty clear lesson. Change upon change has the effect of reopening wounds. Change upon change equals stress upon stress; for when changes happen in close proximity to one another, they can add high levels of unhealthy stress to our lives. (This is true of even the most positive changes, such as an eagerly anticipated move, a longed-for job promotion, a wedding, a new house, or the birth of a baby.) We need to be aware of the danger to our bodies and emotions when we experience cumulative stress. One stressful experience after another takes its toll. Let's give God the time and space He needs to heal us when changes mount up.

Unchangeable Things

One of the most healing things I can dwell on, in the thick of a lot of change, is the unchanging quality of God's love, the unchanging quality of His coming kingdom. There's a kind of balm in the words, "Jesus Christ is the same yesterday, today, and forever" (Heb. 13:8). Unlike all the fads and crazes and political regimes that surround us, He is and was and will be the same.

And I just have to believe that God is using the changes in my life today to chisel away all the temporary, earthly stuff about me so that He can remake me to eternal proportions, in the image of the Eternal One. So although I'm living day to day right now in what sometimes seems to be a world of turmoil and losses and good-byes, it's so good to know that I am on my way to a place where there will be no more death or tears or separations—ever.

When Spike's precious mom, Marjorie, was dying after a massive heart attack, all of us (her children) were allowed to be with her in the intensive care unit. Being there during the last hours of her life was one of the most faith-building experiences I have ever had. Even though her body was dying, we could almost see her spirit growing stronger and stronger, right there in that hospital room.

Even with an oxygen tube in her mouth, drifting in and out of consciousness, she called out the chapters and verse numbers of the Scriptures she wanted to hear. Dutifully, we looked them up and read them aloud to her, amazed by her knowledge of where to find the comfort she needed in the Word of God.

One of these Scripture passages especially stands out in my memory: "All this is indeed working out for your benefit....

This is the reason why we never lose heart. The outward man does indeed suffer wear and tear, but every day the inward man receives fresh strength. These little troubles (which are really so transitory) are winning for us a permanent, glorious, and solid reward out of all proportion to our pain. For we are looking all the time not at the visible things but at the invisible. The visible things are transitory; it is the invisible things that are really permanent. We know, for instance, that if our earthly dwelling were taken down, like a tent, we have a permanent house in Heaven, made, not by man, but by God (2 Cor. 4:15–18; 5:1 PHILLIPS).

Sitting there at the bedside of my brave friend, my mother-in-law, I knew I was watching the most important metamorphosis of her life. Marjorie was being changed right before our eyes from someone earthbound to someone heavenly. Her earthly tent was being taken down, and she was moving into a permanent house that will never change. We knew that as she closed her eyes for the last time, they were fixed steadfastly not on the visible and transitory things of this life, but on the invisible, unchangeable, yesterday-today-and-forever things she'll never have to let go of.

These are the unchangeable things that you and I are being prepared for as we deal with all the changes in our everyday lives. We are being led from glory to glory, through a maze of sometimes unexpected, sometimes inconvenient, sometimes painful changes in preparation for a changeless kingdom where His love will reign forever.

And knowing about this unchangeable kingdom is a real boon when the changes in this world get us down. Dwelling on the unchangeable things makes the changes less traumatic when they come along. Recognizing God's purposes in our

shifting circumstances opens us up to fully experience the
inevitable and ongoing parade of changes we call life.

I consider that our present sufferings
are not worth comparing
with the glory that will be revealed in us.
The creation waits in eager expectation
for the sons of God to be revealed.
For the creation was subjected to frustration,
not by its own choice, but by the will
of the one who subjected it,
in hope that the creation itself
will be liberated from its bondage to decay and
brought into the
glorious freedom of the children of God.

Romans 8:18–20

In the beginning, O Lord,
you laid the foundations of the earth,
and the heavens are the work of your hands.
They will perish, but you remain;
they will all wear out like a garment.
You will roll them up like a robe;
like a garment they will be changed.
But you remain the same,
and your years will never end.

Hebrews 1:10–12

Father, thank You for loving me just as I am.
But thank You, also, for loving me too much
to leave me there.
Help me shake loose from my own selfish agenda,
my own personal preferences and prejudices.
Help me let down the barriers I've built
between myself and Your will for me.

Help me welcome as friends those sometimes
inconvenient, uncomfortable,
and unexpected changes
You bring into my life.
Give me courage to break out of
my comfort zone and follow You.
Change me, Lord, from glory to glory,
as you prepare me for Your beautiful,
unchanging kingdom that is to come.

Amen

CELEBRATE CHANGE

Picture your "comfort zone" as a warm, comfortable cardboard box in which you feel totally protected and secure. Imagine that strong, loving hands have set your cardboard box on a sunny beach where the waves of God's love are beginning to lap up and dissolve it. Outside the dissolving box you can hear the voice of Jesus calling you to follow Him into a new adventure. Gradually your cardboard walls soften and collapse. You can feel the sun on your body. You look up into the face of Jesus and see the love in His eyes. You stretch slowly and stand up. Are you ready to follow?

Now give some time and thought to the following questions:

What is your cardboard box? Is it a location, the respect of certain persons, a certain amount in your savings account?

Whose hands are moving you into a place of change?

To what adventure do you think the Lord might be calling you?

What changes must be made in order for you to follow Him?

I first heard this "cardboard box" exercise used in a teaching by Mickey Smith of Mobile, Alabama.

9

THE TALE OF
THE ORPHAN PRINCE

Claire's chapter about where we really belong

*People are prepared for everything
except for the fact that beyond the
darkness of their blindness there is a
great light. They are prepared to go on
breaking their backs plowing the same
old field until the cows come home
without seeing, until they stub their
toes on it, that there is a treasure
buried in that field, rich enough to buy
Texas. . . . They are prepared for a
mustard-seed kingdom of God not
bigger than the eye of a newt, but not
for the great Banyan it becomes with
birds in its branches singing Mozart.
They are prepared for the potluck
supper at First Presbyterian, but not
for the marriage supper of the lamb.*

—Frederick Buechner

My mama says she just
loves the Bible because it's
so full of quotations. (Actually, I think Mark Twain or
somebody slightly more
famous than Mama said it
first.) But I love the Bible
for its stories. It is full of
amazing, heart-wrenching,
life-changing stories—every
one of them true.

There's the one about the
man who's swallowed by a
large fish and is spit out on
the beach near the city he's
been trying to avoid. Or
there's the one about the
guy who smites all these
other guys with the jawbone
of a donkey, but later gets

his hair cut off and turns into a temporary wimp till his hair grows back and he pulls down a temple on the heads of everybody who ever teased him. Or what about the really old couple who laugh when they get the message that they're going to have a baby, and then, years later, when lo and behold they really do have one, actually name the little boy "Laughter." Then there's the one about the guy who builds a mammoth boat in the middle of a desert because God tells him a storm is coming, which it does, so he gets all these animals aboard and floats around with them while it rains for about a month and a half and absolutely everybody apart from his immediate family sinks and drowns. And that's just for starters!

These stories have it all over fairy tales for my money. If some of the endings fall a bit short of happily ever after, that's mainly because they are more than just true; they are also alive! (John 6:63) Reading them, you realize that people haven't changed all that much, and that God hasn't changed a bit. We're still blowing it, still needing Him. And He's still calling us, drawing us, healing us, and forgiving us, even though we don't deserve it.

Some stories in the Bible are well known. For example, most people (whether they believe a word of it or not) have probably heard the one about Noah's ark. It's world-famous.

But if you took a poll at the corner McDonald's during lunch today, how many people do you think would have heard the one about the orphan prince, Mephibosheth? You probably couldn't even find one person in fifty who could *pronounce* Mephibosheth. Admit it...*you* probably can't pronounce Mephibosheth either.

But this little prince's story is a truly great one. For me, it paints a vivid and colorful picture of God's love for us, His children, in a way that nothing else ever has. That's why I want to share it with you now, in my own way, as something of a spiritual fairy tale.

The Orphan Prince

(See 2 Samuel 4:4 and 9:1–13.) Once upon a time, in a tiny kingdom faraway, there lived a powerful king by the name of Saul. King Saul lived a life of wealth and plenty in the castle with his son, Jonathan, and his grandson, little Prince Mephibosheth.

All the people of the land loved Saul and Jonathan and Mephibosheth. But even more than they loved the royal family, the people loved Jonathan's best friend, David.

Long before this time, when David was just a boy, he had saved his people by slaying a wicked giant who was tormenting the tiny kingdom. But now David had grown up. He was strong and brave and handsome. It was said by many that he was the bravest knight in all of the tiny kingdom. Some even said that David would someday take Saul's place as king.

Now it happened that the tiny kingdom went to war with a neighboring land. King Saul, his son Jonathan, and Jonathan's friend David all strapped on their armor and rode bravely into battle with the other knights of the kingdom. They left little Prince Mephibosheth at home in the castle with his nursemaid, a kind and resourceful old woman who dearly loved the boy.

Every day King Saul and his knights would fight valiantly for the cause of the tiny kingdom. And every day a messenger would bring news of the battle to the castle where little Prince Mephibosheth and his nursemaid were waiting.

For many days the news was good, and for many days the nursemaid and the little prince felt safe in the castle. Then one

day the messenger arrived with tears in his eyes, for the news
from the battlefield that day was very sad indeed.

"You must flee with the child," said the messenger to the
nursemaid. "For this day both his grandfather, King Saul, and
his father, Sir Jonathan, have been felled in battle. Who can
know what fate will befall the little prince when the new king
comes to power? Go at once, without delay!"

Hastily the poor, frightened nursemaid gathered little
Mephibosheth's belongings and prepared to flee the castle,
carrying the little prince in her arms. But in her frenzy, she
accidentally dropped the child on the hard, stone floor of the
castle, badly injuring both of his legs.

How the nursemaid prayed that the child had not been
seriously injured. But alas! Poor little Mephibosheth, son of
Jonathan, grandson of Saul, had been severely crippled. The
orphan prince would always walk with a limp.

Now there was a man named Makir who lived in the land of
Lo Debar, just outside the boundaries of the tiny kingdom. It
was to Makir's home that the nursemaid took the little prince,
and there they stayed in hiding for fear of their lives.

Meanwhile, back in the tiny kingdom, it was decided that the
brave knight, Sir David, should ascend the throne and succeed
King Saul, who had fallen in battle. And so David became
ruler of the tiny kingdom.

What a wise and fearless king he was! He led his people to
many victories and accomplished great things in the land. He
added to his country's wealth and achieved for his people great
stature in the eyes of other kings and nations.

David should have been happy. He had everything anyone
could desire: wealth, power, fame, and the love of his people.
And yet at times, when he was alone, the young king felt a

great sadness in his heart. How he missed his friend Jonathan!

If only Jonathan were here to share all of this with me, David often thought.

Finally David hit upon an idea. He called together his counselors and advisors and put to them a question: "Is there anyone still left of the house of Saul to whom I can show kindness for my friend Jonathan's sake?"

"Well, your majesty," answered one of his wisest advisors, "An old man named Ziba, who was once a servant in the court of Saul, sits every day by the gates of the city, reminiscing about the days when Saul was king. Perhaps he can answer your question. Shall I summon him to you, your majesty?"

"Yes," David answered excitedly. "Bring Ziba here to me at once."

The king's advisor returned shortly, bringing with him a wrinkled and ragged old man who trembled in fear at the thought of being brought before the throne of the new king. He was well aware that it was the custom for a new king to destroy or exile all who had been loyal to the former ruler.

Silence fell over the court as the old fellow at last stood before the throne. King David cleared his throat.

"Are you Ziba?" he asked.

"Y-y-yes, your majesty, sire," the old man croaked. "I am Ziba, your servant."

"Well, can you tell me, Ziba," King David continued, "if there is anyone left of the household of Saul?"

The old man hesitated, still trembling.

"I wish them no harm," the new king added kindly. "I wish, rather, to show kindness to someone of Saul's household, for Jonathan was my dearest friend in all the world."

The old man's expression softened.

"Then I will tell you, sire," he answered. "There is someone—someone very close, in fact, to your friend Jonathan.
Jonathan's son, Prince Mephibosheth, now lives in hiding with
his nursemaid in the land of Lo Debar."

"Mephibosheth? Safe in Lo Debar? Oh, thank God!" King
David exclaimed. "Please, go now and bring him here to me.
And hurry back!"

And so the old man, Ziba, journeyed to Lo Debar, to the
house of Makir, to bring back with him Prince Mephibosheth.

David's heart was brimming with excitement as he awaited
the arrival of Jonathan's son. Years had passed since he had
seen the boy. *How has he changed?* David wondered. *Will he
look like Jonathan? Will he be excited to return to his homeland
after all this time in hiding? Or will he be frightened at being
summoned before the new king?*

Finally, after three long days, the doors to the great hall were
thrown open, and the sound of a trumpet rang out.

"Mephibosheth, son of Jonathan, is here, your majesty,"
announced a loud and droning voice.

Through the massive, ornate doors of the tall-ceilinged hall
hobbled a slender youth in clean but shabby clothes, leaning
on a crude, wooden crutch. Behind him at a respectfully pro-
tective distance followed his kindly nursemaid, who was a very
old woman by now. The young man had handsome features
and a mane of thick, dark curls. His huge eyes were filled with
fear.

"Come closer," said King David, marveling. How like
Jonathan he was!

Slowly and laboriously, Mephibosheth made his way across
the hard stone floors—the very same floors upon which he had
been dropped years before. Finally he stood as erectly and as

bravely as he could before the large, impressive throne—the very same throne upon which his grandfather had once sat.

"You are Mephibosheth?" King David asked.

"I am," replied the youth in as steady a voice as he could muster.

"Don't be afraid," the king said kindly. "I was your father's friend. Indeed, I am your friend. I have never intended you anything but kindness, Mephibosheth, but I had no idea where you had gone. What has your life been like since you left this castle? Where have you been? Please tell me your story."

"The day my father and grandfather were killed, when I was only five, my nursemaid was advised to take me into hiding. We were told that our lives would be in danger, no matter who the next king might be, so she did as she was told. In her haste to depart, she dropped me, and it was then that I was crippled. We have been living in Lo Debar in the home of a friend for all these years, your majesty. We have never known whether it was safe to return to the kingdom of our birth, although we have often longed to."

Tears filled the good king's eyes, and compassion for the child of his friend flooded his heart.

"Why have you brought me here, my lord?" the young man asked hesitantly.

"I wish to show you kindness, Mephibosheth, for the sake of your father, Jonathan. I wish to share with you all that I would certainly have shared with him had he lived. I wish to restore to you all that would have been yours by right had he not been taken from you. I wish to return to you all of the land, all of the possessions, and all of the honor that once belonged to your grandfather, Saul. And I want you to come here to live with me. I want you always to eat at my table with my family."

Mephibosheth stood astonished and unable to speak. He lowered his eyes and shook his head as if to wake himself from a dream far too lovely to be real.

"Why are you so kind, my lord? Why do you bother with someone who can do nothing to repay you?"

"Because Jonathan was my friend, you are my friend," David answered softly. "Because you were his son, you shall be my son. Do you understand?"

Mephibosheth nodded slowly, and for the first time since he had entered the castle a smile spread across his face, erasing the fear and tension from his dark eyes.

Then, with a wave of his hand, the king summoned Ziba once more. The weather-beaten old fellow, moved by the scene he had just witnessed, shuffled forward eagerly to await whatever instructions the king might have to give.

"Ziba," King David said with a note of authority in his voice, "I have given your master's grandson everything that once belonged to Saul and his family. Now I wish for you and your family to return to him and serve him exactly as you would have served his grandfather. You and your sons are to farm the land for him and bring in the crops, so that your master's grandson may be provided for. And you will no longer sit by the gate remembering days of old, but you will once more maintain a position of importance with the royal family. For Mephibosheth, the son of Jonathan, the grandson of Saul, shall now be my own son. And he will always eat at my table."

And so Mephibosheth, the orphan prince who was crippled in both legs, came to live at the castle with King David and was regarded as a prince once more among the subjects of the kingdom. He grew strong and healthy and unafraid, and he came to depend on King David as the father he had lost.

And Ziba and his family farmed his fields, brought in his crops, and served Mephibosheth as they had served his grandfather, Saul. But Mephibosheth always ate at the king's table.

THE END

The Story of Every Believer

I believe the reason I love this story of the orphan prince so much is that this is the story of every believer. All of us were created to be children in the household of the King of kings. Yet all of us have been stripped of this birthright on the battlefield of sin. We've all been wounded and crippled and orphaned by this world and its fallenness.

And in the aftermath of the battle, all of us have found ourselves in hiding, pulling the filthy rags of our shame about us. Knowing in our heart of hearts that we were made for something better, we somehow have been unable to find our way back home.

Then one day, incredibly, we are called—summoned before the great King himself. We come with our heads bowed and our knees trembling, knowing we are unworthy to stand before Him, yet mysteriously drawn into His presence.

Then, tenderly, He speaks our name, and we hear the kindness in His voice. Timidly we lift our eyes, and we see the mercy in His face. We listen in amazement to His words of healing and reconciliation, and we are flooded with an awesome sense of hope. We feel His open arms fold gently about us, and we know that our hearts are finally home.

Home—not because we deserve it or can ever hope to earn it, but because, out of love for the One who stands at His throne and intercedes for us, He delights to give us the kingdom...for free. He restores to us all that was lost, and He adopts us as His very own precious children. What's more, He calls us to a celebration at His table, where we can share in the bread and wine of this glorious new kingdom, the gates of which are now open to us.

My Story, Too

I love this story for very personal reasons, too. I love it because I know it is my own personal story.

I was certainly "in a far country" when I was called before the King. I had been "crippled" in my efforts to escape His rule in my life, and I was living as a spiritual refugee far away from Him. He had sent lots of "messengers" and "servants" over the years to fetch me out of my various "hiding places," but I had stubbornly refused to be rescued.

Then on a January night in 1977, I was able to see that my life was a mess without Him. My own answers were frail and empty. My own ego, which had been on the throne of my life, was an insatiable despot.

Finally, desperate enough and unhappy enough to know my need of the good King, I came out of hiding. Very much like a crippled orphan child, I dusted off my old Bible and "limped" into His presence. Feeling more than a little threadbare, I hobbled before His throne. Trembling and not quite sure what to expect, I looked into His face.

The mercy I found there I will never forget. The grace and love that were waiting for me in my Father's arms have rewritten the story of my life. Since that night, I have lived in His castle, eaten at His table, and known what it means to be a child of the King.

I pray that, in some way, this story of the orphan prince is your story, too. If it is not yet, it is most certainly meant to be.

God, the good King, is waiting to welcome you as His child to your place in His kingdom—a place of safety and peace and privilege that was purchased for you by Jesus Christ. He is waiting to give you your spiritual inheritance—life, hope, joy, even eternity.

Your place is set at His table.

He's restlessly watching the road for the first sight of you in the distance.

He's eagerly listening at the door for your footstep.

Isn't it time you went on home?

But while he was still a long way off,
his father saw him and was filled with compassion for him;
he ran to his son, threw his arms around him, and kissed him.
The son said to him, "Father, I have sinned
against heaven and against you.
I am no longer worthy to be called your son."
But the father said to his servants,
"Quick! Bring the best robe and put it on him.
Put a ring on his finger and sandals on his feet.
Bring the fattened calf and kill it.
Let's have a feast and celebrate.
For this son of mine was dead and is alive again;
he was lost and is found.

Luke 15:20–23

Lord Jesus, I thank You for showing me Your heart of mercy.
Thank You for continuing to seek me out when I was in hiding.
Thank You for constantly drawing me back home to You,
where I may dwell in Your house
and always eat at Your table.

Forgive me for the sins that have kept me from living as a child
of Your kingdom.
I want You to reign in my heart and in my life.
I want You to be in control,
to lead me and to guide me in every large and small
decision.
I give You my life,
and I proclaim You as my King!

Amen

CELEBRATE BEING GOD'S CHILD

If you have never given your life to Jesus, I encourage you to take that step today. It's the most important and life-changing decision you will ever make. Tell Him that you need His forgiveness, His mercy, and His touch of new life. Come into His courts with joy and abandon. Invite Him to reign in your life. There is no greater adventure in this world than to live as a child of the King!

If you do know what it's like to live as God's child, write out a "fairy tale" parable of your own spiritual journey.

Were you a scullery maid who was adopted by the King? Were you under a spell until the Prince of Peace came into your life?

Describe your journey beginning with "once upon a time" and ending with His promise of eternity.

10

SOMEDAY MY PRINCE WILL COME

Karla's postscript about why it's going
to be okay after all

> *What if
> this is
> as good as
> it gets?*
>
> —Jack Nicholson,
> *as the character
> Melvin Udall*

So…now you know.

Now you know why you feel that vague sense of unrest, even if life is good, and things are fine.

Now you know why, every now and then, you wonder, "Is this it? Is this as good as it gets?"

Now you know why so many of us have midlife crises, why we wake up one day and ask ourselves, "What have I really done with my life?"

Now you know why you dreamed of being a princess, and why you keep waiting for the prince to show up.

Now you know why you sometimes feel you don't fit in.

It's because you don't.

It's because you really *are* a child of the King, and this place
is not your kingdom or castle. The old gospel song says it best:
This world is not my home,
I'm just a-passin' through.
My treasures are laid up somewhere beyond the blue.
The angels beckon me
from heaven's open door,
And I can't feel at home in this world anymore.

The Lost Kennedys

I was in elementary school when President John F. Kennedy
and his brother, Robert, were assassinated. My friends and I
were all fascinated with these young leaders, their glamorous
families, and their tragic lives. I was especially captivated by
the drama of Ethel Kennedy, Bobby's young pregnant widow,
left alone with all those handsome children. I cut their pictures
out of *Life* magazine. I even developed a secret crush on
Bobby, Jr. I daydreamed about marrying him and helping his
family not to be so sad.

My friend Cindy also dreamed about the Kennedys when she
was growing up. Cindy, whose own father died when she was
young, often felt sad and lonely, and so she imagined that she
was really a Kennedy, who'd somehow gotten separated at
birth. She envisioned the day when she would be discovered
for the true blue blood that she was, restored to her big,
boisterous, romantically grand family.

Whenever we feel unappreciated, Cindy and I tease each
other about being the lost Kennedys. Just wait, we say; one day
old Ted himself is going to show up on our doorsteps and
whisk us away to Hyannisport to play football on the lawn.

I suspect that most of us have this sense of entitlement deep within us—the feeling that we are somehow more than we appear, that there is something more waiting. This is why we're so fascinated with "royal moments," such as inaugurations and weddings. This is why we keep sending in our sweepstakes entries, why we watch the Miss America pageant year after year. We love to see an average American girl turn into a princess right before our eyes.

When I was little, I would watch those pageants on Saturday night, every year, in my jammies—my hair in pink sponge-rollers, set for Sunday School the next morning. I'd watch the pageant on the little black-and-white TV upstairs, in the dark, all by myself, so I could cry and nobody would see. The minute Burt Parks started singing, "There she is…" I'd flip off the set and jump into bed, pretending to sleep. I could hear my dad switch off the big set down in the living room, turn off the lights, and slowly climb the stairs. He'd stop at the top of the stairs, stand by my door, and softly say into the darkness, "You're *my* Miss America." And I'd lie there in the dark in my pink sponge-rollers, and cry all the more. Everyone needs to feel she's somebody's princess!

Never Enough

This sense of entitlement is okay. It is a part of being created by God, made in His image. It is a glimmer of proof that we are indeed His heirs, His children.

But the Deceiver of this world distorts those feelings, as he does with so many of the good things God created in us. (This is how Satan works, taking what is natural and good, and twisting it until it is distorted and destructive.) He whispers in our ear, "You deserve more," until we are never satisfied. Nothing is ever enough.

Adam and Eve had it all—they lived in Paradise! They had their own little kingdom, custom-made, and the two of them reigned over everything—everything, that is, except for one tree. Satan knew exactly where to strike.

"God is not giving you everything," the snake whispered. "You deserve to have it all." Even Paradise was not enough.

We've all suffered since that day. The voice of the Deceiver whispers to us, even in the best moments, "This is not enough." His voice leads us into all kinds of quests for more—more money, more power, more recognition, more knowledge, more turn-ons, more fun, more freedom—anything to fill that void within that echoes with his insinuations.

Is This All There Is?

In an article entitled "Why We Feel So Bad When We Have It So Good," author and White House speechwriter Peggy Noonan writes: "Somewhere in the Seventies, or the Sixties, we started expecting to be happy, and changed our lives (left town, left families, switched jobs) if we were not. And society strained and cracked in the storm.

"I think we have lost the old knowledge that happiness is overrated—that, in a way, life is overrated. We have lost, somehow, a sense of mystery—about us, our purpose, our meaning, our role. Our ancestors believed in two worlds, and understood this to be the solitary, poor, nasty, brutish and short one. We are the first generation of man that actually expected to find happiness here on earth, and our search for it has caused such—unhappiness. The reason: If you do not believe in another, higher world, if you believe only in the flat material world around you, if you believe that this is your only chance at happiness—if that is what you believe, then you are not disappointed when the world does not give you a good measure of its riches, you are despairing."[1]

Despair haunts us, a shadow lurking at the edge of our mostly sunny lives. We run from it. We work too much, eat too much, drink too much, spend too much, watch too much TV. We do drugs, have affairs, and get divorces to avoid despair. We push our children to overachieve, and we push ourselves as well. We fill our houses with things we don't need; we work overtime for power we don't have—the trappings of royalty. And still we feel estranged from something or someone elusive. We can't put our finger on it. More…there has to be more.

Now and Then

There is more. There is a castle and a throne. "In My Father's house are many mansions; if it were not so, I would have told you" (John 14:2 NKJV).

There is a King in a kingdom. "Then the King will say to those on his right, 'Come, you who are blessed by my Father; take your inheritance, the kingdom prepared for you since the creation of the world' " (Matt. 25:34).

And there is a crown. "And when the Chief Shepherd appears, you will receive the crown of glory that will never fade away" (1 Pet. 5:4).

But these things are not in this world. "In this world, you will have trouble" (John 16:33).

Disappointment results when we expect all that has been promised to us to happen here and now. The Crown Prince himself was an outcast here, a poor man, a laborer with calluses, a servant. An itinerant, not a homeowner. Not an executive. Rarely in vogue. Often rejected. As His fellow heirs, we should expect the same. "If the world hates you, keep in mind that it hated me first. If you belonged to the world, it would love you as its own. As it is, you do not belong to the world, but I have chosen you out of the world. That is why the world hates you. Remember the words I spoke to you, 'No servant is greater than his master.' If they persecuted me, they will persecute you also" (John 15:18–20).

This world is not the kingdom. Not yet. "But take heart!" Jesus assures us. "I have overcome the world" (John 16:33).

The King Is Coming

One day, the Bible tells us, the fanfare will sound. The King will come riding in. And we who belong to Him will receive our crowns. We will reign with Him. The glass slipper will fit.

What do we do in the meantime?

Well, Cinderella had been to the ball. She had worn the dress, the crown, the slippers. She had ridden in the coach. She knew she was the one the prince had chosen. But the next morning, as always, she got up and served her stepmother tea. She picked up her ugly stepsisters' ball gowns. She scrubbed the same floors and washed the same dishes, dressed in the same rags. And just think…all this time she knew there was something more.

And now *you* know.

You know that this house, this furniture, these clothes, this body, this job, these chores—they're not all there is. Every now and then, in your child's laugh, your husband's touch, your friend's smile; in a sunset or a rainbow; when a neighbor comes through—every now and then you get a shining reminder of a kingdom that is beyond the here and now.

There is more than this life. This is our promise, our hope. And this is why we sing.

Do you remember the Bible story about Paul and Silas, imprisoned in the town of Philippi for healing a girl in Jesus' name? God sent an earthquake to get them out of jail. But before that, beaten and chained and stuffed in that musty dungeon, they were praying and singing praise to God (Acts 16:25). Ever wonder what they were singing? Maybe, "I've Got a Mansion Just over the Hillside." Or perhaps, "The King Is Coming." One thing is for certain: Their sights were set on something far beyond their present circumstances.

And you and I, wherever we find ourselves at this moment— mopping floors, wiping noses, typing letters, closing deals, checking out groceries—can sing. Just close your eyes, smile to yourself, and hum, "Someday, My Prince Will Come."

Because, you know, He will.

---

[1] Noonan, Peggy, "You'd Cry Too, If It Happened to You," *Forbes* (New York: September 1992).